DATE DUE

OCT 1 6 1990		
NOV 2 3 1990	FEB 1 9 1996	
May 4, 9?		
	OCT 1 1 1996	
JUL 1 1 1991		
SEP 1 4 1991	JAN 4 1997	
OCT 8 1991	JUL 2 8 1997	
JUL 2 1992	JAN 2 1 1998	
JUN 2 4 1993	FEB 11, 1998	
SEP 1 6 1993		JUN 0 9 1998
JUL 2 6 1994	AUG 0 4 2001	
AUG 16 94 K		
OCT 1 1994	JAN 0 2 2003	
JUL 0 6 1995		

#47-0108 Peel Off Pressure Sensitive

TOTAL TENNIS

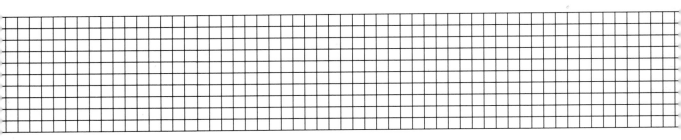

Also by Peter Burwash and John Tullius
Tennis for Life

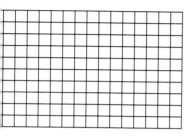

TOTAL TENNIS
A Complete Guide for Today's Player

PETER BURWASH AND JOHN TULLIUS

PHOTOGRAPHS BY TED WASHINGTON

MACMILLAN PUBLISHING COMPANY
NEW YORK

COLLIER MACMILLAN PUBLISHERS
LONDON

Macmillan Publishing Company
866 Third Avenue, New York, NY 10022
Collier Macmillan Canada, Inc.

Library of Congress Cataloging-in-Publication Data
Burwash, Peter.
    Total Tennis/by Peter Burwash and John Tullius.
       p. cm.
    Includes index.
    ISBN 0-02-620401-0
    1. Tennis. 2. Tennis—Coaching. I. Tullius, John. II. Title.
GV995.B838   1989
796.342'2—dc19   89-2837   CIP

Macmillan books are available at special discounts for bulk purchases for sales promotions, premiums, fund-raising, or educational use. For details, contact:
    Special Sales Director
    Macmillan Publishing Company
    866 Third Avenue
    New York, NY 10022

Diagrams on pages 128 and 194 by Jim Mintz

10 9 8 7 6 5 4 3 2 1

Printed in the United States of America

To my wife, Lynn,
for her patience and understanding.

Thanks to Ted Murray for his faithful help with the editing.

—P.B.

CONTENTS

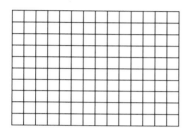

SET TWO

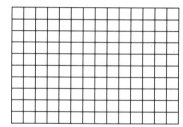

PLAYING YOUR OPPONENT'S COURT: THE STRATEGY FOR THE TOTAL GAME   119

SET THREE

OFF THE COURT   213

TOTAL TENNIS

INTRODUCTION

It's a whole new ball game in tennis today. Players from club hackers to the top ten are simply hitting the ball harder. Everyone knocks the cover off the ball now. I played the professional circuit in the sixties and early seventies and faced all the great players of the day, including Rod Laver, the dominant player of the era. I can say without doubt that the top five hundred players in the world today, almost to a man, hit the ball harder than Rocket Rod did.

You don't appreciate how hard Ivan Lendl or John McEnroe or André Agassi hit until you're actually standing right there trying to deal with the immense pace on their ball.

The women's game has accelerated dramatically as well. The biggest woman's serve in the sixties was Margaret (Court) Smith's, which came in around 90 miles per hour. This year's women's winner at the National Fast Serve Contest was clocked at 119!

The men mainly responsible for this revolution in pace are not Björn Borg or Jimmy Connors or Ivan Lendl, but inventors like René Lacoste and Howard Head. Lacoste is the man who introduced the first metal racquet—the Wilson T-2000. That's the racquet that Connors used to win over one hundred pro tournaments in his illustrious career. Head introduced the first oversize racquet—the Prince Classic.

These revolutionary racquets allowed players to hit the ball twice as hard with half the effort, an improvement in equipment which has created a phenomenal advancement in the game. Personally, I can hit the ball 30 to 40 percent harder than I ever could when I was a young circuit player twenty years ago. And almost all of that power has come from the size and shape of the new frames, not because I got stronger.

But there has also been a tremendous change in the people playing the game. The tennis boom brought money and widespread media exposure to the game, and along with it came a tidal wave of new players. Tennis went public. No longer was it hidden behind the ivied walls of country clubs, a game played mostly by the rich and famous.

Today, everybody's doin' it.

This enormous influx of players means the quality of the

tennis athlete has improved exponentially. You have literally thousands of great athletes playing tennis now, guys who are big and fast and strong and can really pulverize the ball. Consequently, the game of tennis is more of an athletic contest than ever before.

But with the addition of all this power, something has been lost—namely, understanding. The players of today simply don't understand the game as well as players in the past.

That's right. Even most touring pros do not understand the game they dominate. That statement may come as a shock to a club player or an up-and-coming junior who idolizes the pro tennis player. They closely watch how he hits the ball and what he does on the court. They'll switch their TVs to Wimbledon and watch Boris Becker crush his way to the title and think, Yeah, that's the way tennis is supposed to be played.

But let me tell you something. Becker, in the early stage of his career, had a very poor understanding of the game of tennis. He won almost exclusively on sheer talent and brute strength. If you're going to emulate Becker, you had better have his awesome abilities and his gargantuan power. The truth is, Becker has not yet really lived up to his incredible potential because of his lack of understanding.

Boris is not just a well-known exception either. Having coached many touring pros over the years, I have found that very few of them have a solid understanding of the game. They don't know when and where to hit certain shots and they have no real understanding of court positioning. They hit shots that put them out of position and don't know how to take advantage of their opponents when they do get them in a vulnerable spot. They just hit the ball.

Now, if two players with awesome ground strokes and no knowledge of the game or the court it's played on are pounding away at each other, then knowlege doesn't really make a lot of difference because both players are blundering around the court. But a player who is very inferior physically and strokewise can beat a much superior player if he understands the game. You see it all the time, in fact. A good senior player can often dominate a good junior player. The junior hits the ball twice as hard as the old guy and covers three times as much court, yet walks away with a loss.

At some point in his career the junior will begin to hit the ball so hard and be so physically superior that he will be able to overcome his dumb shots, poor percentages, atrocious court positioning, and total lack of knowledge of the game. He'll simply blast the old guy off the court. But it takes an incredible edge in talent to overcome such ignorance.

Today's players are obsessed with power. They think they

can ignore percentages by hitting great shots all the time. No player in the world has ever been able to do that. Lendl couldn't. The "old" Lendl would just hit harder and harder, and if that didn't work he'd call it a day. His only "strategy" was to overpower his opponent. If he couldn't do that he had no alternative.

Ivan's game changed when he hired Tony Roche, the great Australian left-hander, to coach him. And what big change did Roche make in Lendl's game? Well, he taught him how to hit the ball softly. Instead of belting a topspin on every service return, Ivan now often chips the ball low and softly to the opponent at the net. This usually elicits a weaker volley from his opponent, and *then* Ivan will go for his big shot.

He's also changed the pace in baseline rallies. Less and less does Ivan find it necessary to always hit a hard shot from the baseline. When the time is right, yes, he will really crack one. But only when it's worth the risk.

Only after Ivan learned to take pace *off* the ball did he become number one in the world and win his first grand slam championship. He went on to take three French Open and three United States Open titles, and he's twice been a finalist at Wimbledon.

Boris Becker, on the other hand, skyrocketed all the way to number two, but he has since fallen as far down as number seven. His slide has been blamed on everything from the loss of his coach to spending too much time with his girlfriend, but that's not the problem.

You cannot be number one in the world strictly on talent. Until Boris learns to really play the game of tennis, he'll struggle. There are too many talented players fighting to be number one who have taken the time to truly understand the game.

Like Ivan Lendl.

So who is the player of the future? Well, he's the guy who truly understands the game. Not just how to belt the ball, but how to use all the different speeds and spins and placements to beat his opponent. Oh, he'll be able to whack that ball, but he'll also know when to unload and when to use the other tools in his bag to win. The player of the future will do it all at all speeds. In other words, he'll have a total understanding of the game. He'll be a complete player.

THE IMPORTANCE OF UNDERSTANDING

What does this mean to the average tennis player though? Should everybody's goal be to become a complete player? Yes. If you're like almost every other tennis player, you've reached a plateau on which you're stuck. No matter how hard you practice, no matter how many lessons you take, you're stuck on that level. Most likely you're on the intermediate level of the typical club player, somewhere near the top of the C or B ladder. But you're not good enough for the A's or to play in local open tournaments.

You probably really tried to get better for a while. You went to a few pros in town, and they all corrected your stroke "flaw." And that was guaranteed to put you on that mythical A level. But it never did. That's where a significant number in the tennis-teaching profession have let students and players down. Many pros give beginning and intermediate lessons, but they can never seem to get you past that intermediate level. Once you get the ball over the net, you're more or less on your own. So after five years of frustration you probably gave up. You figured, That's it! I guess I've reached my potential—the eternal B-level player relegated to the same old boring doubles match every weekend.

Well, there is a way to get unstuck! No matter what level you're on, from beginner to tournament player, you can start improving immediately by gaining a total understanding of tennis.

We've all seen lessons where a pro stands next to his shopping cart feeding balls to a student and correcting any flaws in his or her forehand or backhand. But where and when does a player use those strokes? And for what reasons?

A lesson is often a highly segregated hour so divorced from the game of tennis that you have trouble ever using what you learn. A pro will try to teach you the "perfect" backhand, which the pro himself may admit takes years (and years) to master. Even though it may be a classic stroke designed to really pulverize the ball, you usually give up and go back to your old ways because what the pro is teaching you just won't apply to your game for a good five years. The lesson, then, may be totally useless.

It's like being given one piece of a jigsaw puzzle and being expected to know what the puzzle looks like. The task is impossible. That's why you're given a picture of the completed puzzle on the box—so you can see the overall picture. You may not be able to fit the piece right into the puzzle, but you've got a pretty good idea where it goes. That's what I want to do with tennis—show you the entire picture right from the beginning so you can piece it together that much faster. So you can see where you are and where you're going and plot out a plan for your improvement.

You must see the entire picture if you want to get to the next level. There are so many variables in the game of tennis—different climatic conditions, different spins, different surfaces, different balls—that you must become aware of them all in order to understand what is holding you back.

For example, you may believe you're suffering from a snake-bite, but if you actually have cholera all the antivenom in the world is not going to help you. Similarly, you may think your lousy backhand has been your problem all along, but it may be that you have horrible court positioning and you're forced to run a mile to even get to the backhand. Simply understanding court positioning may catapult you over an opponent you have never been able to beat—overnight. Now wouldn't that be nice?

The next time you go out and play after you have read this book, you may get an inkling of what's really happening on the court. Then, if you're smart, you will come back to the book, read some more, and go out and experience and experiment. I guarantee that if you do this, in three to six months you will have revolutionized not only your game, but what you understand about the game of tennis. You may, in fact, really see the total game for the first time.

SET ONE

THE BALL'S IN YOUR COURT:
THE FUNDAMENTALS OF SOUND STROKES

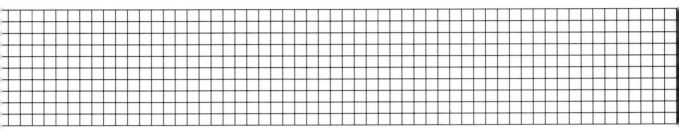

PART I
THE REAL FUNDAMENTALS

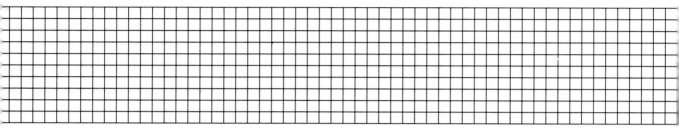

CHAPTER 1

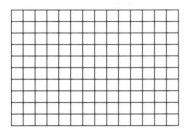

THE FIRST FUNDAMENTAL—UNDERSTANDING THE CONTACT AREA

FORM IS NOT A FUNDAMENTAL

Most instructors start with the teaching of "classic form" because they think it's one of the foundations of the game—the natural place to start building a good tennis game. But classic form is really just a preconceived idea of what someone should look like while hitting the ball. Form is not a fundamental at all, it's a style. And like all styles it changes with time.

Form is nothing more than what the great players over the years have found practical. Then, of course, the rest of the tennis population copies the champions, and five to ten years later everybody's got a "Graf forehand." Or to be more accurate, their forehands are in the same style as Steffi's.

The point is, form did not come first. Stroke production is a matter of style, and style is secondary to function, to what actually works. When the score goes up it says "6–2, 6–1." Period. It doesn't say "6–2, 6–1, but Chris sure had a nice-looking backhand." Looking good doesn't win matches.

There are dozens of right ways to hit all strokes. But strangely, the Eastern forehand was almost the only forehand taught for the last forty years in clubs all over America. It doesn't take a keen eye, however, to see that most of the great forehands in tennis today are semi-Western forehands like Graf's and Lendl's and Becker's. Over the years there have been great forehands and backhands hit in all kinds of ways. The key here is not to copy those strokes, but to find the fundamentals common to those great shots.

John McEnroe has a unique style of play that's all his own. So it appears that his game is not fundamentally sound simply because he doesn't look like anyone else who's ever played. You'll hear coaches all the time say, "Boy, he's a great player, but I'd never try to teach my students to play that way."

That's where they are wrong. McEnroe is an ideal model for tennis players because the fundamentals of what he does on the court are perfectly sound. You just have to know what to look for. If you want to be a great player, copy John's fundamentals, *not* his style.

In short, the fundamentals of sound stroking are understanding the contact area, good balance, and use of the nonracquet hand. And Johnny Mac's strokes are built solidly on these foundations.

UNDERSTANDING THE CONTACT AREA

There are three parts to the typical stroke—the backswing, the contact area (the area where the racquet and ball are in contact), and the follow-through. By far the most important of these three is the contact area.

The entire game of tennis, quite logically, centers around the moment when the racquet strings contact the ball. That's the contact area. Everything—backswing, follow-through, footwork, concentration, preparation, strings, shoes, you name it— is secondary to that moment. You can have the greatest-looking backswing and the greatest-looking follow-through, but if you don't have control of the racquet in the contact area, you won't hit the ball effectively.

HAND-EYE COORDINATION

Some players have trouble with the concept of the contact area, not because they don't understand its importance, but because they have poor hand-eye coordination.

How many times have you heard a club-level player say, "Geez, I blew that last shot because I wasn't watching the ball!" But the reason he missed the shot had nothing to do with whether he watched the ball or not. I have never once had a student swing on the backhand side when the ball came to his forehand. If a ball comes to the forehand side, the biggest klutz in the world will swing on the forehand side 100 percent of the time. Why? Because he already sees the ball. The reason he doesn't hit it is because he hasn't lined it up properly. In other words, he lacks the proper hand-eye coordination, and that's what he has to develop.

There are pros who tell the student: "Watch the ball hit the strings!" Well, that's impossible. Ophthalmologists tell us we begin to lose sight of the ball approximately six feet before contact. So how do you hit the ball? You line it up—just as someone who catches a ball or Frisbee behind his back cannot see it all the way to his hand, but must instead line it up.

I was doing clinics for servicemen once in Okinawa and made the statement that in an hour I could teach anyone to hit a tennis ball back and forth across the net twenty-five times in succession. This guy came up to me afterward and challenged me.

"My wife is so uncoordinated that we have the only dishwasher in Okinawa because she broke most of our plates washing them by hand, and we live in a one-story house because she can't walk up a flight of stairs without tripping. She is not spastic, she's just got no coordination."

An excellent way to test your coordination and at the same time practice dual vision is to have a player toss two balls to you out of one hand. Try to catch one ball in each hand. Then, as you progress, try catching the balls with your hands crossed.

Once you have learned to catch the balls, practice catching one ball and hitting the other. This will teach you to split your vision and is a good preparation for learning triple vision (see p. 122).

And, believe me, she was very uncoordinated. To this day she's the only person I've tossed balls to who failed to hit with even the frame. And I've developed the kind of toss that, if you don't move your racquet, the ball will hit it. If I tossed low, she'd swing high. If I tossed high, she'd swing low.

So we spent two days on hand-eye coordination drills. We tried to zero in on simple aspects—just bouncing the ball off her racquet where she couldn't miss—all the way through to the tougher drills, where she'd hit it off the edge of her racquet.

Two nights later, in front of a thousand people, including her husband, she and I hit some balls. After 15 or 20 returns in a row her husband began to lose his mind. He actually stood up when we got to 40 or 50, and as we kept going he started clapping like a total crazy man. This is quite a famous story now, because she and I ended up hitting 142 balls in a row over the net!

This is an important point. People assume they're uncoordinated and that's it! They figure they just can't learn. But, believe me, hand-eye coordination can be taught and developed. I have never failed to teach hand-eye coordination to anyone, although it is different for each person.

First of all, test your own or your children's hand-eye coordination. The following drills will help a player to develop hand-eye coordination.

SELF-VOLLEY DRILLS

1. Begin simply by bouncing the ball in the air on the racquet strings with a forehand grip. This is called a self-volley.
2. Then self-volley, alternating with hitting the ball on the racquet frame's edge. Then walk doing this drill. Then jog.
3. Next self-volley on the backhand, then on the edge, alternating. Then walk. Then jog.
4. Then hit a forehand self-volley with backspin. Then walk. Then jog. Then try it on the backhand side.

DRIBBLING DRILLS

1. Dribble the ball at waist height. Then walk while dribbling. Then jog.
2. Dribble below knee height. Then walk. Then jog.
3. Bounce the ball off the ground using the edge of the racquet.
4. Dribble on the backhand side while using a forehand grip. Then walk. Then jog.

CATCHING DRILLS

Place the ball on the racquet strings and toss the ball into the air. Then catch the ball without letting it bounce on the strings by reaching up toward the falling ball and cradling it on the racquet as it descends. This is called a cradle catch. Do it on the forehand side, then the backhand side.

Playing catch with a Frisbee is also a great way to develop hand-eye coordination. Try catching the Frisbee on the run, or behind your back, or whatever trick comes to mind. All these will further develop your hand-eye coordination.

The best way to correct problems with the contact area is to play minitennis. In all the years I've taught tennis, my teaching methods have constantly changed, but the one thing that has survived is minitennis. The basic concept of minitennis is to keep the ball within the confined space of the four service boxes. The first thing, of course, that everyone wants to do is whack the ball back and forth from the baseline because that's the way the pros do it.

But think about this. In New York City a study was conducted of average club players during an hour of tennis to determine how much time was spent picking up balls and how much time was spent actually playing tennis. It was found that the average players spent fifty minutes picking up balls and ten minutes playing. And in New York City, where court time often runs over fifty dollars an hour, that's awfully expensive for ten minutes of playing time!

● ● ●

The great advantage of minitennis is that anybody can immediately begin to hit a lot of balls over the net. I've taught two guys confined to wheelchairs who have hit 154 balls in succession over from the baseline because they started with minitennis. I've also taught a three-year-old and a man of eighty to hit 100 balls in a row over the net in their first hour of tennis through the concept of minitennis. But if you start out at the baseline, you may never hit a hundred in a row over in your life.

And for all you big hitters who figure minitennis is "puff-puff" tennis, best suited for little kids and old men, swallow your pride, because when I first saw minitennis it was being played by two Australians named Laver and Roche.

The idea is to learn to control the ball by first playing down-the-line minitennis, then crosscourt minitennis, and then eventually full-court minitennis, using the entire minitennis area to move your opponent around.

Minitennis teaches the idea of the game. The focus is not on backhand or forehand, but on court awareness. You learn tennis movement, which *is* minimovement, small steps taken in a confined space. Tennis, contrary to how most beginners gallop around the court, is not the hundred-yard dash. Also in minitennis you're learning to control the ball, which means dealing with the obstruction of the net and playing in a confined area.

And, perhaps most important for the beginner, there is no overload on the mind in minitennis. A big complaint of all beginners trying to learn to hit the ball is, "I've got so much to remember!" There's a great mental overload in trying to learn

strokes—turn sideways, change grips, step forward, keep your racquet head down, up, sideways . . . help! The player ends up doing everything but hitting the ball. Trying to remember more than one or two things at a time causes confusion, frustration, and a lack of concentration. So move off the baselines, the free-way of tennis, and come up to the side streets (the service boxes) and play a little minitennis. Remember, before you become a good tennis player (before your muscles memorize the new move-ments involved in tennis), you'll have to hit quite a few balls. And if you spend fifty minutes every hour picking them up, it may take forever.

Minitennis singles and dou-bles is one of those great exercises that is not only fun, but also very practical. In singles you use only the two service boxes on each side, but in doubles you can use the alleys as well. Two basic rules: no hitting hard and all players should concentrate on backspin. (The emphasis in miniten-nis is on ball control, and backspin is your control spin.)

THE MAIN PROBLEMS WITH CONTACT AREA AND HOW TO OVERCOME THEM

The main mistake a typical player will develop in hitting the ball is overcomplicating the path that the racquet takes. As he swings he does funny things with his arm or wrist instead of simply realizing that the racquet head is an extension of his hand.

That's the advantage of playing minitennis. There is no backswing or follow-through in minitennis, so you must concentrate simply on making contact with the ball. One of the first things I do, in fact, when someone is too preoccupied with backswing and follow-through, is take away their follow-through. Immediately they begin to hit the ball in the center of the strings. As a practice exercise just freeze your swing at the point of contact and concentrate on pointing your strings toward the intended target. This gives you a feel for the presentation of the racquet head.

Another useful method to ensure that you are pointing the racquet strings toward your target is to keep your wrist and racquet head moving together. A slapping motion is created when the racquet head flies ahead of the wrist as you swing. So if you think "wrist and racquet head together" as you point the strings, it will control the racquet head.

Another way of visualizing this is thinking "palm forward." No matter how you swing, the racquet head will only go where the palm goes. That's common sense. So if you zero in on the palm as you swing, you will know where your racquet face is pointing. On the backhand think "knuckles forward."

Also, if your strokes are crumbling (or you never had any strokes to start with), slow down your swing. We all want to crunch that ball, but when you're not hitting well, one of the most fundamental corrective techniques is to pretend your arm is in a slow-motion movie. In this way your mind can begin to perceive what your body is up to. It's simple enough, but how many times have you seen a player who has lost his touch start to hit harder and harder trying to get it back? It's obviously foolish, but that mixture of panic and pride just won't let him slow down.

Another method you can use to practice control of the racquet head is to try choking up on the racquet handle, because the farther down you grip the racquet, the greater the weight at its head and the greater the tendency to slap at the ball. If you move your hand up the handle, you'll have more control over the racquet head and a better understanding when you return to the full grip.

The technique I emphasize the most, however, in correcting problems with the contact area is to firm up the wrist. More than any single factor, a firm wrist enables the player to control the path of the racquet head. When your wrist is floppy, flying around out of control, your palm is also out of control. Your wrist is the link between your body and your racquet, and if you have a weak link you have a weak (that is, inconsistent) shot.

The proper technique for hitting with a firm wrist is not, as many believe, to squeeze harder with your entire hand, because your index finger and thumb have little to do with controlling the wrist. Only the last three fingers of the hand are connected anatomically with the set of tendons that control the tightening of the wrist. So if you concentrate on squeezing those three fingers, the wrist will firm up nicely.

The only time you want a loose wrist is in an extreme emergency, when you want to get the ball over any way you can. A flexible wrist can be very useful at those times.

THE SEVEN TIMES YOU DON'T TAKE YOUR RACQUET BACK

Wherever tennis is taught you'll hear the phrase "racquet back." That seems to be the most frequently used instruction for beginning tennis players—"Get your racquet back!" And that one phrase has probably destroyed more potentially good tennis players than any other piece of advice. The racquet-back–follow-through brand of coaching ignores the most important part of the game—the contact area, or hitting the ball.

In fact, there are seven times when you do not take the racquet back:

1. On a hard-hit ball
2. On a volley
3. On a half volley
4. On a ball hit right at you
5. When you're slow physically
6. When you're slow mentally
7. When you're slow physically and mentally

ON A HARD-HIT BALL

The first thing most players do when the ball has been blasted at them is to try to hit it back even harder. But most players just don't have time on an extremely hard-hit ball to get their racquet back. Instead, just present the racquet face to the ball and let the natural rebound of the strings provide the pace on the ball. The ball will go back with plenty on it, and best of all, it will probably land in. But if you take a huge backswing, the ball may be past you before you swing at it. At the very least you'll swing late and the ball may end up three courts away.

This situation frequently occurs when you play an opponent who hits much harder than you're accustomed to. Instead of trying to hit as hard or harder than your opponent, you should simply use the stronger player's pace to your advantage.

ON A VOLLEY

In most cases it's natural to bring the racquet back on the volley because for so long almost every pro kept yelling "Racquet back!" That's why so often a player has problems learning to volley. He is programmed to bring his racquet back, so as soon as he sees the ball his immediate instinctual reaction is to take a big backswing. Whether the ball is in the air, on the ground, whether it's coming fast or slow—back goes his racquet. That's why I teach contact area first and introduce the backswing later.

Think of all the people who get their racquet back regardless of the shot. Even someone as phenomenally successful as Chris Evert. Yet how well does Evert volley? To this day you'll still sometimes see Chris swinging on a volley. You only take the racquet back if you have time, and on the volley you usually don't have time.

On the volley you don't need to supply a lot of power, so you don't need a big backswing. First of all, there is a tremendous amount of rebound in the strings, so you've got plenty of power without swinging. Secondly, in the ideal volley position (halfway between the net and the service line), a player is only fifty-two feet from the baseline and a put-away volley to a side T (the T-shaped area formed by the service line and the sideline) will travel only twenty-five to thirty feet. If you're volleying at the net, then, there's no question that you'll have enough power. It's a question of control—will you be able to keep it in?

ON A HALF VOLLEY

The half volley is a ball you hit just after it bounces, so it is basically a defensive shot. No one wants to hit a half volley. Usually a player is forced into that situation because his opponent has hit a strong shot at his feet. If your opponent hits a soft floater, you can step back and take it on the full bounce or move up quickly and take it in the air. So if played correctly, you should only be hitting half volleys off balls that are hit fairly hard, and therefore just the natural rebound off your strings will supply all the power you'll need to hit the ball deep.

Players who learn the phrase "racquet back" when they first start playing tend to take a big backswing on their volley because the first thing they do is take their racquet back. But on most volleys no backswing is needed. To correct the "racquet back" habit, stand with your back against a fence or pole. This forces you to limit your backswing and teaches the feeling of a compact volley.

19

ON A BALL HIT RIGHT AT YOU

It's difficult for many players to accept that if the ball is hit directly at you, you're in a defensive position and you should simply try to block the ball back with a minimum amount of backswing. When a ball is hit right at you, you're also extremely vulnerable. That's why in doubles, for instance, it's smart to aim for the opponent's right hip (if the player is right-handed), because that's where he's most vulnerable.

WHEN YOU'RE SLOW PHYSICALLY OR MENTALLY OR BOTH PHYSICALLY AND MENTALLY

These apply to beginners as well as athletes playing at the French Open who are in the fifth set of one of those clay-court marathons and are physically and mentally fatigued. Those pros will begin to hit the ball with an extremely abbreviated backswing because their legs have had it and their arms weigh a ton and they'll do anything they can to just get it back. So they zero in on contact and live off their opponent's pace.

Beginners are usually slow physically because they're not reacting properly to the ball coming at them. And they're slow mentally because they're confused by the new situation—they have so much to remember. So, the best advice for a beginner or someone who is fatigued or just doesn't move well on the court is simply to concentrate on the contact area. It's not necessary to take a big backswing.

RACQUET PREPARATION

Instead of "racquet back," I use the term "racquet preparation," which carries the implied understanding that there are many times when you hit a ball without taking the racquet back. Basically, you should prepare your racquet according to the speed of the ball. The slower the ball, the farther you can take your racquet back, because the purpose of the backswing is to add power, to hit the ball harder. And if the ball is already coming hard, there's no need to add more pace to it. That's the essence of racquet preparation as opposed to racquet back. In other words, you should take your racquet back when you have time—which may be on every shot if you're playing a weak player.

When I play a strong player I can usually take the racquet only about three-quarters of the way back at most. Now imagine most beginners or intermediate players who have all those things to remember. Sure you can take a big swat when someone is tossing balls to you or when you're playing the club pushover. But anyone who understands tennis is not likely to feed you those setups in a match.

Your racquet preparation is also determined by the circumstances. For example, if the court surface is very fast concrete, you should shorten your backswing, whereas on clay (a slower surface) you usually have more time before you swing. Consequently, you see a lot of clay-court players with long, looping backswings. Also, if there's a heavy wind playing tricks with the ball, or if you're playing under lights and the visibility is poor, or if the balls are new and therefore very quick, then again you should shorten your backswing.

Finally, if you're playing an opponent who always takes his racquet back immediately on every shot, try hitting the ball very slowly. His muscles will be so tense from holding the racquet back for so long that the trigger will go off just ahead of time and he'll end up hitting crosscourt on every shot. It is a very fine bit of timing we're dealing with here, and it really doesn't take all that much to throw off a solid hit. So, if you change up speeds frequently on a "racquet back" player, you'll often force him into mishitting the ball.

THE FOLLOW-THROUGH

The final element of a typical stroke is the follow-through, and contrary to popular belief, it has nothing to do with hitting a good shot, because by definition the follow-through begins the moment the ball leaves the racquet strings. The only purposes of the follow-through are to prevent injury and to complete a natural motion.

It's very dangerous to stop your swing immediately after hitting the ball. If you stop your swing abruptly, the result can often be a muscle pull or tendon strain—in other words, common ailments such as tennis elbow.

The correct follow-through is a simple, commonsense thing. Usually problems only begin when you do too much with the follow-through—wrapping it around your neck or rolling the wrist over at the end to try to put all sorts of fancy spin on the ball. Basically, just let your arm finish the movement freely and the follow-through will occur naturally.

CHAPTER 2

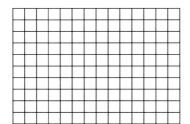

PROPER BALANCE

The most difficult task in tennis is getting from one place to another. If you can get to the ball, I can teach you to hit it. Hitting the ball, as I've said before, is not all that difficult. But getting to the ball so that you're ready to hit a good shot *is* difficult.

Just because you're fast does not mean you can get to the ball effectively; in fact, the beginning and the end of the run are the most important parts of getting to the ball, not the run itself. First of all, the player who gets a quick start has anticipated what his opponent will do and, in most cases, could probably get to the ball on crutches. And secondly, once you get to the ball, speed is meaningless. The important question becomes, are you balanced?

BALANCE VERSUS FOOTWORK

Forget footwork. All this elaborate teaching of footwork does nothing but confuse people. It puts too much of a mental overload on you. You can move around a lot, turn sideways, move your shoulders and feet in a certain way, and yet you may fail to accomplish your original goal—to hit the ball over the net.

I knew a pro who actually painted steps on the court to show you where each foot should go as you set up for a shot. That's ridiculous! Who really has the time in a match to calculate exactly where to put each foot? Besides, no two shots are ever hit the same.

Footwork is secondary to balance. In fact, footwork is just a technique for maintaining balance while hitting a shot. The concentration of a player who learns footwork, therefore, is all wrong. The mental focus is directed to the feet when it should be directed to the belly button, which is the center of gravity— at least, in males. (The center of gravity in women is slightly lower, which gives them better balance. The higher center of gravity in males gives them better speed.) So it's not footwork you want to learn at all, but balance.

A body is in balance when the center of gravity is directly over the base, which, of course, is the feet. To determine the size of your base, simply take a piece of chalk and draw a rectangle on the ground around the heels and toes of both feet so that it covers the little area that you stand in. That is the area over which you must align your body.

It's natural to be in balance. That's why players will do such strange things with their feet on a tennis court in order to maintain balance. They look uncoordinated and awkward, but, actually, they're doing what nature intended—staying in balance. You'll see players spin around, go up in the air, lean backward, anything they can do to avoid falling over. These are all natural compensations the body makes to stay in balance. So people are, by nature, balanced. Only very infrequently do players actually fall on the court, because they know instinctively, long before they fall, that they're off balance. That great computer, the mind, instantaneously cries for help, and the body makes the proper adjustments.

How do you prevent yourself, then, from going through all those unnecessary motions in order to maintain your balance? First of all, your feet must be a reasonable distance apart so you can create a base of balance. Then be sure your head does not lean outside that base. Once it does you're off balance.

The best technique for creating better balance is simply to bend your knees. Your base is a very narrow rectangle, much wider than it is long, and therefore very unstable. It is very easy to lose your balance. But by dropping your navel down (bending your knees) you lower your center of gravity, thereby creating a more stable base. You become like one of those inflatable dolls with the sand in the feet—almost impossible to knock over. That's why a player who is aware of the balance factor will drop his center of gravity if he's losing his balance.

A beginner often makes the mistake, however, of bending at the waist, thus throwing his weight outside the base of the feet. So he's out of balance before he begins to move. Is it any wonder that he has trouble getting to the ball?

DRILLS TO STRESS BALANCE

1. A good technique to learn better balance is to concentrate on just one part of your body. For instance, put all your weight on your lead foot and bend your lead knee at a ninety-degree angle as you hit (or you can also lower your back knee). This focuses your mind on the task of maintaining the proper balance throughout a point.

2. Play without a racquet, catching the balls a friend hits to you. This eliminates any distractions created by the racquet or setting up to hit the ball. You can concentrate on getting to the ball in balance.

3. Freeze after you hit each shot and see if you can place your racquet flat on the ground between your feet while maintaining your balance. This is a handy check to see if you have the proper base for good balance.

4. Try hitting everything with two hands—both the forehand and backhand. This forces you to set up closer to the ball, in a more balanced position.

5. Study yourself in a balanced position—feet apart, knees bent, head and navel over the top of the base—and create a visual picture of it. Practice it in front of a mirror until you know what it feels like without looking.

ON YOUR TOES

Good players keep their heels off the ground throughout a point. They're on their toes (that is, the balls of their feet).

You always move the heel before the toe when running. So if you're already on your toes you eliminate that extra movement. And that's all the difference in the world.

People usually play flat-footed because they're out of shape. They can last only five to ten minutes on their toes. But it's all a matter of conditioning. You've got to get in condition to play a good game of tennis, which means playing on your toes the whole time you're out there. If you can't go an entire hour on your toes, book a court for twenty minutes or half an hour and go all out on your toes for that length of time. If you do, in a week or two you should be able to last the entire hour. You'll probably be dead tired, but you will improve your game at least 50 percent by just doing that one thing.

See, when you get lazy on the court, everything starts to fall apart in your game. Have you ever played a very slow doubles match where the other players just weren't very good? What happens? You fall asleep and before you know it you're playing as badly as the other players. Now, if you're in a game in which the other three players are all better than you are, you usually play the best tennis of your life. Why? Because you know you've got to go all out just to keep up. You're on your toes, ready for every shot.

ARE YOU READY?

Most players are not ready for the next shot. They're running one way or another and have not gotten themselves into the proper position on the court or are off-balance. In fact, the biggest weakness in most players' games right up to the top level in the world is that they relax between shots during a point. They hit the ball and stop to see how it goes. Then they wait for their opponent to hit his shot before they make another move. *A good player works just as hard between shots as he does when he's hitting the ball.* Maybe even harder!

The main objective is to get your balance before the opponent hits the ball so you're ready to go in any direction. That's where the "ready hop" comes in.

A ready hop is simply a little hop you take the instant *before* your opponent hits the ball. Hop and land on the balls of your feet, with your head over the top of your feet. This assures that you are balanced and ready to go in any direction to get the next shot.

Not only will the ready hop get you ready for whatever comes off your opponent's racquet, it can give you the ability to explode to the ball. If you take your ready hop and you're in balance, almost nothing will get by you.

BODY WEIGHT AND POWER

Another myth about footwork is that you should step into the ball, thereby transferring your weight into the ball for greater power. But the transference of body weight on ground strokes has nothing to do with power. Our company of teaching pros, Peter Burwash International (PBI), conducted a test in Los Angeles. Using a radar speed gun, we compared the speed with which a player could hit a forehand with a closed stance (the front foot "stepping" into the ball) and an open stance (the front foot to the side of the back foot). We found virtually no difference. In fact, many people could hit slightly harder with an open stance.

Now, what's significant about this test is that on an open-stance forehand your weight transfer is actually going toward the sideline, not toward the net. It's physically impossible to get your weight going toward the net, because from the hips down you're stationary. Therefore, it's your arm that supplies most of the power. Even on a closed-stance forehand your weight transfer (from the back foot to the front foot) should occur before the ball is contacted, not during the stroke.

There are pros who teach that weight transfer should occur simultaneously with the contact of the ball and the swing of the arm. Their students have incredible problems with timing, particularly in special circumstances, such as when the ball takes a bad bounce or in a heavy wind or when playing a junk-baller or a spin artist. If you try to time your weight transfer to coincide with the exact moment you contact the ball and the ball goes off course even the slightest bit, you'll be incapable of making the necessary adjustments. It's far more difficult to suddenly change the direction of your entire body than to make a simple arm or wrist adjustment.

What creates the ball's pace is timing, and good timing means being able to connect with the ball in the center of the racquet at exactly the right instant for maximum power and control. A so-called heavy ball is created by timing, not weight transfer, as is evidenced by someone like John McEnroe, who has small biceps but can hit one of the fastest serves in the world because of his superb timing.

The classic example of how timing influences speed occurred in Los Angeles, where PBI held a fast-serve contest. We had several players from the National Football League and two 85-pound twelve-year olds, and the kids could serve faster than the 250-pound football players. The football players could pick the kids up with one hand, yet their serves were, on the average, ten miles per hour slower.

HITTING OFF BALANCE

There are many times in a match when you will not be able to maintain balance and still hit the ball. Your opponent has you climbing the fences, chasing balls, or twisting and turning to hit overheads. So what do you do?

The key to hitting an effective shot when off balance or on the run is the dissociation of the upper part of your body from the lower. The biggest mistake you can make while chasing the ball at full speed is to let the momentum of your feet transfer to your racquet head and overpower the ball. Instead of racing fifty feet to get to the ball and then hitting it fifty feet out, your idea should be to dissociate your arms from your feet. Run as hard as you can to get to the ball, but don't let your body transfer its foot speed to the arm at the point of contact. You should have fast feet and a slow arm.

If you're off balance, you're in an extremely weak position. You're on the defense and your objective should be to neutralize the opponent. Most players, however, try to do too much with the ball. For some reason they think they should hit their best passing shots when they're off balance. On off-balance shots, however, contact area is critical, because when you're off balance you're in an emergency situation. And in emergency situations you should always limit the motion of the racquet face. Don't get fancy; don't try a shot you haven't made in ten years.

HITTING ON THE RUN

Hitting on the run presents its own problems. There are many times on a running shot, for instance, when you don't take your racquet back at all because you can run faster by pumping both arms. Players conditioned to run with their racquets back can't move as well because there's a natural drag on the body when running in that position.

When you are forced wide to hit a shot, it's important to try to stay within the point of contact. A player who takes an extra step or two beyond that point (known as recovery steps), inevitably puts himself in trouble for the next shot.

Sometimes the ball is hit so wide in the court that there is no way you can stay inside the point of contact, stop, and get ready for the next shot. You're forced to hit the ball on the run. When that happens, go for the outright winner! When running sideways, however, swing your racquet straight ahead toward your opponent's side of the court to compensate for the sideways motion of your body.

If you're running laterally, the tendency is to hit a short ball. You'll tend to compensate for your lateral movement by swinging your arm toward where you came from, so that on a forehand your racquet will end up over your left shoulder (right if you're left-handed). This creates a very short contact area and therefore a very short ball.

Don't let the lateral direction of your feet influence the direction in which your palm moves. The correction is to exaggerate the palm-forward movement in order to lengthen your contact and hit deep.

RECOVERY STEPS

Of course, if you're a smart player you'll try to stay balanced so that you're never forced to run beyond the point of contact to recover your balance. If you're off balance as you hit the ball, however, you'll need what are known as recovery steps, and that will put you out of position for the next shot.

Basically, recovery steps are used to stop your forward momentum so you don't hurt yourself with an abrupt stop. At times they are necessary, but many players use recovery steps on every shot, making it much more difficult to get back into position and leaving much more court to cover.

The idea is to get to the ball in plenty of time to stop your momentum at the point where you intend to make contact with the ball. Instead, many players time their run to intercept the ball just as it gets to where they plan to contact it. This means they're forced to run several steps beyond the point of contact to slow themselves. If you take two recovery steps, it will take you two more steps just to get back to where you contacted the ball, where, in fact, you should have stopped in the first place. Which is why professionals learn to slide to the ball when playing on clay. The tricky footing of the surface does not allow for quick stops, and by sliding they can go full speed and yet still decelerate and brake themselves so they aren't forced to go beyond the point of contact.

When you're forced to use recovery steps and your opponent is at the net, you must either lob in order to buy more time so you can get back into position, or you must try to end the point immediately by going for the outright winner. Curiously, these two shots are seldom attempted. If your opponent is at the baseline, a looping semilob is effective since it also gives you time to recover, is relatively easy to control, and cannot be easily smashed away by your opponent.

CHAPTER 3

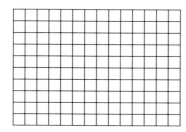

THE USE OF THE LEFT (OR NONRACQUET) HAND

The final ingredient in a good stroke and the key to self-correction is the use of the left hand. Basically, the left hand (for a right-handed player) has four functions:

1. To change grips
2. To rest your racquet hand
3. To keep the racquet head up
4. As a guide hand on the racquet

USING THE LEFT HAND TO CHANGE GRIPS

It is impossible to show every player the backhand grip that's right for him. There is total individuality to the grip. It changes from player to player because there are so many variables involved. For example, everyone's fingers are different lengths and their hands are constructed differently, Also, there are many types, shapes, and sizes of racquet handles.

You will see dozens of books and thousands of pros, however, who teach that you can find the backhand grip by placing the V between the thumb and forefinger down the left edge of the racquet handle. Or something like that. But that does not take into account round or oddly shaped racquet handles or the myriad variations of the human hand. That's why there's so much confusion. A player will be stuck with an improper grip for years and, therefore, will be unable to present the racquet face to the ball without being forced to compensate by bending his wrist into some awkward and weak position.

Another important point is that if you're right-hand dominant (that is, you change grips with your right rather than your

Placing a thumb up the back of the racquet handle sometimes gives the beginning player a little more stability on his backhand, but it also leads to tennis elbow and poor stroke production. For the best results and an injury-free future, wrap the thumb around the racquet handle. You can usually tell if your opponent has his thumb up the back of the racquet handle because he will stick his elbow out as he swings. An excellent way to exploit someone who uses this grip is to hit the ball low.

left or nonracquet hand), you will lose your feel for your grip changes (forehand and backhand) periodically. It will come and go whether it's every day, every week, or every month.

For this reason I haven't actually shown anyone the backhand grip in years. I prefer to train students to adjust the grip with their left hand. I have a student set the racquet up with his left hand so the face is perpendicular to the ground. Then I have him hit several balls, adjusting the grip accordingly until it feels both strong and comfortable.

There is one very important point I'd like to make. When changing to the backhand grip, never place the thumb behind the racquet handle for added support. This severely limits your progress because it inhibits the rotation of your wrist necessary to execute many of the shots used by more advanced players. It also tends to make you poke at the ball. You'll tend to stick your elbow out toward the ball and use the elbow as the pivotal point of your swing—which is a great way to get tennis elbow. The pivotal point of your backhand stroke should be your shoulder, and for very sound anatomical reasons. Your shoulder is a rotational, or pivotal, joint, while your elbow is a bendable joint. When you lead with your elbow instead of your shoulder, you're asking your elbow to act as a rotational joint—that is, it rolls over, stretching ligaments and tendons designed only to bend. Before you know it you're wearing one of those little white

support bands around your elbow. On ground strokes your thumb is basically a nonfunctional digit. It should simply be wrapped around the racquet handle.

USING THE LEFT HAND TO RELAX
THE RACQUET HAND BETWEEN SHOTS

Closely related to the grip change is the relaxation of the right (or playing) hand between shots, because common sense will tell you that you can't change grips without releasing your hold on the racquet. Even more important, however, the left hand enables you to rest the right hand between shots.

Many players use a "long-intensity grip," which means they grip the racquet very tightly long before they've hit the ball and long after. This creates undue muscle fatigue. Instead, a good player uses a "short-intensity grip," which is loose between shots, and supports the racquet briefly with the left hand. This technique keeps the right hand completely relaxed between shots and thus ready to supply power when it's time.

You may have difficulty remembering to use your left hand to rest your racquet hand between shots, so a little gimmick to use (in practice only) is to wipe your racquet hand on your shorts before every shot until you get comfortable with this technique.

The use of the nonracquet hand is essential for a good volley. Players who do not use the nonracquet hand to support and guide the racquet head often have an unstable, "floppy" wrist, which leads to a big backswing and a tendency to slap at the ball when volleying. Another common mistake is to place both hands together at the bottom of the racquet handle. Players tend to take a bigger swing at the ball when they have their hands in this position because they have little control of the racquet head.

A beginning or intermediate player tends to drop his racquet head down around his knees between shots because his hand gets tired holding it up. If he'd use his left hand for support, though, his racquet hand would not get fatigued. Getting your left hand up toward the top of the handle with the index finger actually touching the strings is important for a balanced racquet. You don't carry a long pole by grabbing it at one end with both hands; you put one hand farther up the pole to create a better balance. There's a substantial amount of weight pulling the racquet head down, and if you have your left hand down next to your right, over the course of a match your racquet can begin to feel as if there's a lead weight at the end. That's why the wrist gets sloppy and the shots begin to fly all over the place.

USING THE LEFT HAND AS A GUIDE
FOR THE RACQUET FACE

The most important use of the left hand is as a guide for the racquet face. The left hand can be the perfect computer for your strokes. It can tell you how far from the body the racquet head is, how high or low it is, and how far back you've taken it without looking at the racquet or taking your attention from the court, the ball, or your opponent—where it should be. The left hand can tell the brain, which tells the racquet hand, what the angle of the racquet head is, and this bit of anatomical teamwork gets the ball over the net.

Some players are born with the ability to hit the ball in the center of the strings and some are not. Most are not. I've had a problem all my life with hitting the ball on the frame. I did experiments in which I put black ink on balls and painted my racquet frame white, and I'd color almost the entire frame black during the course of a set just from hitting the frame so much. But as soon as I began using my left hand, this problem suddenly disappeared.

CHAPTER 4

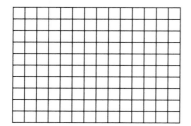

YOUR DEFENSIVE FOUNDATION

TENNIS IS A GAME OF EMERGENCIES

To truly understand the game of tennis, you must start with the fundamental understanding that tennis is a game of emergencies. Thus, in order to be a good tennis player, you've got to have a solid defensive foundation. See, the better players force you into either physical or mental emergencies. It's how well you deal with those emergencies that determines how well you're going to do in tennis.

Good players have sound defensive skills, and the extraordinary ones, like McEnroe and Wilander, have great defensive skills. You have to be able to react to those times when your opponent forces you into emergency situations. Against some players you are almost always on the defensive, while against others you are almost always on the offensive. But there has never been a match when a player has been on the offensive the entire match. Lendl could play a raw beginner and at least a couple of times that beginner would hit a shot—probably off the frame—that would force him into a defensive position.

Most teaching pros show you the accelerator and say, "Take off!" They've forgotten all about the brakes! They teach as if tennis were played on a freeway where everyone gets out of your way no matter what you do. Now, does that sound like your last match? If it does you've got to stop playing the old lady next door. Because if you're playing someone on your level he'll probably get you into trouble, put you into one emergency situation after another. And if you play up a level or two there will be a siren going off in your brain almost constantly.

When I played Arthur Ashe at the U.S. Open for the first

time I was on a pretty good winning streak. I had been on the international pro circuit for a time, and I was consistently getting to the quarterfinals. I even had a few championships under my belt. I knew Ashe was a great player, but I was confident as we were warming up that if I just could get my game going I'd give him a tough go.

But I'd never yet played anyone of Ashe's caliber (he was in his prime and ranked number two in the world), and after the first point I knew I was in over my head. It wasn't just that everything I hit came back; every ball Ashe hit put me in trouble. I'd serve and after that I was immediately in trouble. It was the first time I had experienced such constant, intense pressure during a match. Almost every shot was an emergency situation.

When a car goes out of control, that's an emergency. When your game falls apart during a match, that's an emergency too. How do you deal with that? If someone hasn't shown you how to downshift or use the brake, how will you know what to do? It's almost impossible.

Everything doesn't always go according to plan out on the court. If you're a beginner the ball may get behind you because you were slow off the mark or you reacted late. But a pro will react on time and the ball may still get behind him. Why? Because his opponent created an emergency situation, put him under pressure. In fact, the better you become, the more relevant emergencies become, because when you challenge better players they have the potential to put you in more trouble.

Everyone meets his match. There are only a few players in the world who can put Lendl in trouble, but it happens to everybody. If it happens to Ivan Lendl, it will happen to you. So, if players at that level meet their match, imagine how often you will meet yours. There will come many times on the court when you're totally out of control—when you can't get set, you can't get prepared, you're one step behind, always struggling. Why worry about learning how to set up to hit an ideal forehand when you'll only get that opportunity 10 percent of the time? Why not learn how to deal with emergency situations?

The idea is to get the ball back and at the same time neutralize your opponent, which will get you out of trouble so you can go back on the offensive on the next shot or the shot after that. The prime example probably is when a player is at the net and he's got you in big trouble. Rather than trying to blast a ball or lob (which won't get you out of the defensive spot), a good idea is to chip. Make the opponent hit another soft volley, which gives you time to get back into position. You may get a weak ball in return, and suddenly you're in command of the point.

One problem many players have, however, is accepting the

fact that they're on the defensive. Their attitude is, I'm going to make an offensive shot no matter what. Their opponent has just crunched a volley to the corner, and they run like a maniac just to get it. Then they try a topspin passing shot that they've never even made in practice. And they expect to win matches!

Tennis is a game of emergencies. There will be many times during the match when all you can do is get your racquet on the ball. Use your wrist rather than your arm to try to get the ball back. A quick wrist flick is really all you've got in these desperate spots, and the player who has learned to use his wrist to hit the ball when necessary can get himself out of a lot of trouble spots.

MINIMUM POTENTIAL

There are a thousand things that can go wrong in a match. The ball can take a bad bounce, or hit a line and skid, or you may simply judge the ball poorly. You can never really be sure what will happen next on the court. So you need a backup in order to get the ball over when things go wrong. That backup, that ace in the hole, that little bit of stroke insurance, is minimum potential.

Minimum potential is simply the understanding that a racquet possesses in its strings a great potential for power without swinging. If you're forced into an emergency situation because you're on the run, or the ball is blasted at you, or the wind whips the ball off course, you won't have time for a big swing. Just stick your racquet out with the strings pointing in the direction you want the ball to go, and the minimum potential, the natural rebound of the ball off the strings, will supply almost all of the power you'll need.

Remember, the court is only seventy-eight feet long and the ball weighs only about two ounces, so you need only a minimum of effort to hit the ball over the net. In baseball you can hit a home run, and in golf a long drive is often a bonus. But in tennis there's no reward for hitting the ball a long distance. If you understand minimum potential, you realize that no swing at all is necessary or even desirable on many shots. All you really have time to do in many situations is present your racquet face to the ball and try to get it back over the net. Your opponent often supplies the power, and you can use your opponent's pace to your advantage.

Another thing to keep in mind is that the understanding of the potential of the racquet is a basis of good ground strokes. The racquet will do the majority of the work for you. You don't need a huge backswing and windup to hit the ball hard.

EMERGENCY FOOTWORK

When you've given a player a midcourt setup and he's going to blast it away, you've got to be extra ready to take off. When you know you're in big trouble and the opponent will probably hit a winner on the next shot, you've got to gamble. Choose one side or the other, then break to that side just before the opponent hits the ball and hope you've guessed right. It is a mistake to hold your ground and try to get to the ball after he's hit it. You cannot cover the whole court when a player has a putaway. You've got to guess and hope. If you just hold your position, there is usually no hope.

PART II
MANAGING YOUR STROKES

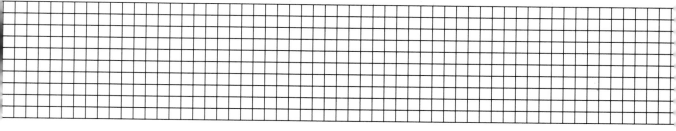

CHAPTER 5

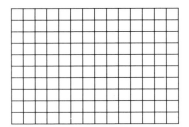

HOW TO BECOME YOUR OWN COACH

WHY YOU WANT TO BE YOUR OWN COACH

One year at Wimbledon, after I'd bombed out in a very early round, I sat with Rod Laver in the grandstands and we got to talking as we watched a match. I asked him, "Who do you go to when you're in trouble?"

In his typical, matter-of-fact Aussie tone he replied, "I go to myself."

Whether you want to or not, you must eventually learn to coach yourself. When you're in the middle of a match and you're hitting too long or too short, what do you do? Or what if your opponent suddenly starts rushing the net, volleying like a madman, and you find you can't hit a passing shot that day? Or you can't hit deep, or your serve has crumbled? Who do you go to for advice right there in the middle of a match? Your opponent? No, you've got to go to yourself. Your goal should be to become a self-sufficient tennis player so you can win even when your strokes desert you.

I stress commonsense tennis—in other words, doing what's practical. There are things you must do to hit successful strokes, but the mechanics of the swing are relatively simple. If you're way out of position and you have to run a mile just to get to the ball, and then you try some shot you couldn't make in a dream, all the textbooks in the world are not going to help you. What you don't seem to understand is that even Steffi Graf would have lobbed that shot.

Hitting the ball is not such a difficult task. If you'd stop trying to do nine hundred things at once, you'd probably hit plenty of winners. The key is to simplify, to use your common sense. You must have simple adjustments so that they can be called on in a pressure situation when the mind can usually handle only one thing at a time. Most important, however, you must understand the cause and the result of what you do with your racquet in order to make the proper corrective adjustments. For example, if I ask a club-level player at the end of a match to tell me what his mistakes were, he usually can't do it. He'll say, "Oh, I guess I didn't watch the ball." Or a player will come to me and say, "I'm having trouble with my backhand." So I'll ask, "What's wrong?" And he'll usually answer, "I don't know. I just can't hit it."

Most players have certain identifiable weaknesses. They make the same specific errors over and over, but they haven't really thought about what they're doing wrong, about whether the ball is going long or short or wide. The problem is that most players only look at a shot closely if it's good. They bask in the glory of their great shot. And if they flub one they close their eyes in agony before the ball has even landed. The key, however, to correcting your own game is watching what happens to your own errors. What was the result of that horrible backhand? Did it go into the net? Did you hit it on the throat of the racquet? Remember, before you can correct your mistake you have to know what went wrong.

My aim is to show you how to *be your own coach*, so if your game falls apart you can quickly and systematically analyze your problems right on the court. In order to correct your strokes, however, you've got to build them on solid fundamentals of understanding. The three fundamentals of sound stroking—contact area, balance, and the use of the left (or nonracquet) hand will help you build your understanding of how to hit the ball. Along with this general understanding of the stroke, I will show you how to develop "simplicity checkpoints," which correct the particular, idiosyncratic breakdowns of your individual stroke. Inevitably, everyone develops his or her own style, and with it his or her own particular problems. The three fundamentals of a stroke are the general understanding, and the simplicity checkpoints are the particular correction.

But let me stress again, the basis of self-coaching is common sense. I can't tell you what you should do in every situation. You must take the information that I supply and develop the corrections and techniques that will work for you. In a match you must learn to use your head, because it's the only one you've got. Then if it gets down to the crunch in the last set, like Rod Laver, you can go to yourself for help.

CHAPTER 6

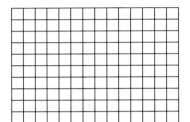

THE FIVE DIMENSIONS OF A STROKE

Just as you are overcoming the physical problems of hitting a ball by mastering the three fundamentals of a sound stroke, you should also be developing your understanding of what to do *with* the ball. There are five basic things to think about when you hit a tennis ball. They are what I call "the five dimensions of a stroke": (1) *getting it in*—get the ball over the net and into your opponent's court any way you can; (2) *direction*—gain control over whether you hit the ball crosscourt or down the line; (3) *depth*—be able not just to hit the ball to the opponent's baseline, but to any depth; (4) *spin*—you can perform miracles with spin by making a ball curve in or hop over your opponent's head. Control of spin separates the beginner from the advanced player); and (5) *speed*—anybody can blast the ball, but the good player can control the ball at any speed.

In the practice session before a match, the five dimensions help you gauge your potential that day. I remember one year at the United States Open Jimmy Arias walked into the press conference after a tough loss and said, "I couldn't hit my backhand today."

That's simply not true. Believe me, he could hit his backhand that day. If we held a gun to his head and said, "We're going to shoot you if you don't hit one hundred backhands in a row in the court," he'd be able to do it. He probably wouldn't be able to murder the ball, but he would get it in. What he meant was that he couldn't hit a backhand in the fifth dimension—he couldn't hit it *hard* and get it in.

That's what the five dimensions are all about. They are a yardstick, a way of measuring your game that day. If you've got number five power that day, go for it. But how about the bad days?

I watched Arthur Ashe, who had one of the best serves ever, completely crumble on his serve on a very windy day. Another time I saw Rod Laver, who had one of the greatest overheads in the world, completely whiff on his overhead in two consecutive games in a big championship. Both Ashe and Laver were number one in the world at the time I saw them. The point is the greatest shots in the world can vanish at any time.

So I try to teach a player what to do when his game falls apart, as it inevitably will. Once your game falls apart your natural ability doesn't count for much. Your feel for the game and how you like to hit the ball are worthless.

The five dimensions are a simple way of determining what you can and can't do that day. The problem is you may have a backhand that feels great one week and you may get the idea that you now have a terrific backhand. But every shot at some point in time is going to fall apart. Don't confuse your potential—what you can do on your best day—with what you can do right now. Sure you've hit some backhand topspin passing shots. But can you do it against a hard deep volley to the corner on the run? Probably not.

● ● ●

Practice is the time to develop your strokes—not during a match. When practicing, you should follow a certain developmental progression for each stroke:

1. Getting it in
2. Direction
3. Depth
4. Spin
5. Speed

I don't mean to imply that you can't practice all five dimensions at the same time, because in fact many of these dimensions overlap. In other words, concentrate on dimension 1, getting it in, until you can get it in most of the time, then concentrate on dimensions 2, 3, 4, and 5 in order.

A major stumbling block for most players is their inability to understand that tennis is a game of control, not power. Power or speed is the last stage in the development of a good tennis player. And even at that stage, the player must develop *controlled* power, because power does not come from swinging harder. It comes from better timing (which takes time to develop), and timing is the ultimate control of the racquet.

To get the ball in the court, the first thing you must do is contact the ball. Beginners always take up their positions at the baselines as they see the pros do on TV, and they seldom hit more than two balls over the net in a row. Most of their time is spent picking up balls, and then they complain that they never get enough exercise when they play tennis.

If this is your problem, come in closer and play minitennis. Develop some feel for the contact area and learn to deal with the obstruction of the net and playing within a confined area. From there you can expand. But give yourself a chance to succeed. If you can't get the ball over the net, lower the net. If you can't get it back over the lowered net, hit it back and forth over a line. But don't go through the frustration of taking your racquet all the way back and complicating what's already a difficult task. There is no form involved in just getting it in.

To get to a decent level in tennis, contrary to popular opinion, is not that difficult. To get really good—yes, that's a difficult job. But just to have some reasonable success presents no real difficulty. Of course, if you think you should be on the pro tour in two years and you play twice a week, then you're not being realistic. But you can play a decent game without a lot of horrible frustration if you'd just forget about hitting the perfect shot and instead concentrate on just getting the ball in.

That's why tennis is often much harder for the good athlete in the beginning than the nonathlete. An athlete wants to play like Lendl in two weeks and ends up overhitting and trying too hard to look good. In other words, he tries to do things he can't do right away and becomes frustrated.

Many of my beginning students will sigh in relief when I tell them it's all right to try anything they want to get the ball over the net. One of my first drills, in fact, with beginning women who cannot hit an overhead is simply to have them run back and flip the ball over their heads, because many women beginners have weak, floppy wrists. So this flipping motion is quite natural for them. It is also very effective and helps build their confidence.

Also, I encourage squash or racquetball players to take those natural wrist shots and use them whenever they can in tennis. A squash player can handle emergencies quite nicely, though he has trouble with a medium-paced ball right down the middle. What I'm suggesting is that you take your natural strength and make it into an effective shot.

Take what you can do and develop it into a strength. For example, the wrist flick is a very natural thing. There isn't a person in the world who starts playing tennis with a naturally firm wrist. So if you're extended to the end of your reach or the ball gets behind you, by all means do what comes naturally—flick your wrist! Form won't help you in those situations, and besides, that's what Graf or Lendl would do with these emergencies. The difference is that unlike a beginner, Lendl does not find himself in that situation on nearly every shot.

DIRECTION

You can't be satisfied forever, though, with just getting the ball over the net. Your goal should be to have the ability to hit any part of the court, but especially to the seven target zones—the two deep corners, the two side T's, the two dropshot areas (the two short corners where the sidelines meet the net), and down the middle.

DEPTH

Most players think hitting for depth means hitting the ball deep in the court, so that the ball lands just inside the baseline. But just as there are many depths in a swimming pool, there are also many depths on a tennis court. There are many times when you don't want to hit the baseline. For instance, you may want to hit short in order to bring a good ground-stroker into the net or to move a slow player around. Or if you aim for the baseline when your opponent is at the net, you may never see the ball again, because that's often a setup for a player at the net. The idea is to make a player at the net play a low shot so he's forced to put an arc on the ball to get it over the net.

You don't necessarily hit the ball deeper by swinging harder, which is a common misconception. Another misconception is that a good shot skims just a few inches over the net. In fact, when his opponent is at the baseline, a pro tries to clear the net by three to seven feet on normal ground strokes—three on a fast court, seven on a very slow one. This fact usually comes as a big surprise to most club players. Good tennis players don't worry about low net clearance; they concentrate on depth. There is a direct relationship, however, between clearance of the net and depth. A line drive that just skims the net often falls short, and, more often than not, balls aimed three to six inches over the net never make it over at all. It's not how close you come to the net that's important, it's where the ball lands. A ball that clears the net by six feet, if it has any speed at all, must land deep in the court. So it follows that you can add depth simply by hitting the ball higher over the net.

Perhaps the easiest way to increase depth is by opening up the angle of your racquet face with the left hand. To hit shorter, close your racquet face.

Another way of getting greater depth is by lengthening your contact area. Contact area is defined as the area in which the racquet and ball are in contact with each other, and lengthening or shortening the contact area is one way of increasing or decreasing depth. Your contact area can be lengthened, then, by pushing forward with your palm (and thus the racquet face) through the contact area.

The best way to lengthen the contact area is to stand with your feet a reasonable distance apart and bend your knees. When you bend your knees the center of gravity lowers, thereby creating better balance. And if you widen your base while bending your knees, you create a *potentially* longer contact area. This enables you to stroke forward a longer distance with your palm through the contact area without losing your balance. Conversely, if you stand straight up or with your feet close together, you limit your contact area, which results in a shot that is often nothing more than a slap.

Hitting with an open stance also tends to shorten the contact area. Your balance zone with an open stance is only the length of your foot, and therefore a player who hits a forehand or backhand with his body facing the net often hits short because he has a very limited potential contact area.

I'm not advocating hitting every shot with a closed stance, but the great open-stance forehand players like Wilander and Borg learned to bend way down to increase their potential contact and concentrated on hitting with an elongated contact area—in other words, they pushed their palm forward through the ball.

You should basically avoid hitting open-stance backhands because the forearm is not usually strong enough on a backhand to maintain an elongated contact area. However, sometimes it is necessary; for example, when the ball is hit directly at you and you don't have time to move. In those cases, remember to use minimum potential.

DRILL FOR VARYING DEPTH

Try to land the ball on the service line, then the baseline, remembering to change the depth for each shot. In other words, avoid hitting two balls short or two long in a row.

A more advanced technique for varying depth is through the use of spin. There are only two things that cause a ball to land in the court—gravity and spin. Beginners use gravity to make the ball literally fall into the court. If they want the ball to land deeper, they hit it harder. Advanced players use spin.

Spin creates friction with the air, and friction slows an object down by creating drag, or resistance. It's the difference between skiing on powdery snow and skiing on ice. The ice offers very little resistance, and the skier flies uncontrollably down the hill. Without spin the ball flies out of control. If you add spin you slow the ball down—you add control. Less spin gives less control; more spin, more control. That's why the pros can hit so hard and keep the ball in. They utilize spin.

Spin opens up a whole new world of creativity. You can hit harder, more difficult angles (for example, you can't hit effective side-T shots from the baseline without spin) and you can vary depth. More spin gives more drag and less depth; less spin gives less drag and more depth.

Knowing the results of different spins enables you to better exploit your opponent's weaknesses. A topspin shot bounces high, and most players don't like a high ball to their backhand. A backspin bounces low and therefore must be hit to clear the net, and a ball being hit up is more easily volleyed away (see Chapter 21, The D–N–O Theory).

When explaining how to hit spin I prefer not to go through any elaborate scientific explanations of vector forces. I've found those scientific explanations are often confusing for students. So, let's keep it simple. In most cases, when trying to hit with spin, prepare the racquet the same for both spins. For topspin finish with the racquet on edge—that is, perpendicular to the ground. If the racquet face finishes open to the sky, you will hit backspin.

Perhaps the key ingredient to hitting spin is a firm but flexible wrist. Gone are the days of racquet-back flat ground strokes. This is the age of spin. It's important to realize the range of rotation the wrist must go through in order to use spin successfully. The palm must rotate under for a backspin forehand, and for a backspin backhand the knuckles rotate upward. There's no way to hit a backspin ground stroke unless you rotate the wrist and racquet face to an open position. Or, if you're starting with a completely open racquet face, to hit a topspin you'll have to rotate the wrist in the opposite direction so the racquet face is closed.

There are pros who advocate putting your thumb up the back of the handle for a firm, locked wrist; but this makes it impossible to hit shots such as a drop shot, which demand a full rotation of the wrist to properly execute. An iron-locked wrist is neither natural nor correct. You need some freedom of movement. Instead, the proper technique to achieve a firm but flexible wrist is to tighten the bottom three fingers of the hitting hand.

SPEED

The last element of the ground-stroke progression is speed. But speed does not mean just hitting the ball hard. It means all speeds. Can you hit the ball slow and easy as well as hard and fast? In order to be a good tennis player, you must be able to do both. There are many times in a match when a slowly hit ball is the best shot—even on a passing shot.

It may feel great to hit the ball hard, but tennis is a game of restrictions imposed upon you by lines, obstacles (the net), and an opponent, who is trying to make the restrictions and obstacles that much greater. That's why I emphasize the phrase "racquet preparation" rather than "racquet back." The only purpose of a bigger backswing is to hit the ball harder. I don't want speed to be a factor until a player can handle speed.

EXPERIENCING THE TWO EXTREMES

An excellent drill to learn to control speed is to experience the two extremes. For the first ten minutes hit the ball as hard as you can. Just nail it—gamble completely on every shot. Then for the next ten minutes hit everything softly with touch and placement in mind. This drill impresses upon you the slim possibilities of getting the ball in if you hit it as hard as you can. Also, after experimenting with these two extremes, the medium-paced, steady shot seems simple.

CHAPTER 7

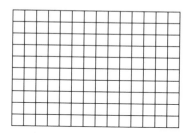

MANAGING YOUR GROUND STROKES

SIMPLICITY CHECKPOINTS

Simplicity checkpoints are the tools that enable you to correct the particular problems that you're having with your strokes. If you can't correct yourself you have no future because you can't have a coach on the court with you in a match. First of all, it isn't practical, and secondly, it's against the rules. And since by the nature of tennis your game is certain to fall apart at least for a while in every match, you must know how to correct it as it goes. Or else you're through for the day.

Your game may fall apart or your opponent may create another problem for you to overcome, but you will never be caught making the same old mistake over and over if you've learned simplicity checkpoints and how to be your own coach.

SIMPLICITY CHECKPOINTS DURING A MATCH

As I've discussed, simplicity checkpoints are simple pieces of advice you can give yourself as a guide to correct your stroke problems. Your approach to self-coaching during a match must be very simple or you'll confuse yourself, and before you know it nothing will be going over the net. You don't want to be out on the court during a match trying to learn how to hit a backhand volley; that's for your practice sessions. You should concern yourself only with what you can do to correct your errors and have a few checkpoints you can fall back on if one of your strokes begins to falter.

Simplicity checkpoints for match situations are inevitably something each individual must develop for himself. By using a number of the simplicity checkpoints I offer to develop strokes in practice situations, a player should be able to find one or two catch words that can serve as checkpoints when a specific stroke gives him trouble in a match.

Specific problems with a stroke are usually chronic—they show up over and over again. And they're likely to show up most in pressure situations. That's when a simplicity checkpoint developed by working on that chronic problem can come in very handy.

Some of my own personal checkpoints have pulled me through one emergency after another. On the forehand I think about squeezing my bottom three fingers to reduce my tendency to slap the ball. On the backhand I think "left hand." On the serve I think "hit up" because I'm not very tall and I tend to hit into the net when pressured. And on passing shots I try to relax because passing shots usually create pressure situations.

Remember, in a match, forget how your strokes look. Developing strokes is a matter of practice—a great topspin backhand takes years of work and talent. In other words, you've got the strokes you showed up with. So, concentrate during a match on the simplicity checkpoints that work for you and on the three fundamentals of sound stroking—contact area, balance, and the use of the left (or nonracquet) hand.

SIMPLICITY CHECKPOINTS DURING PRACTICE

I don't believe in teaching students exactly how to hit a ball. If you want someone to show you the so-called classic strokes, there are a hundred books out there. But let me stress this: there is no right way to hit a ball. Look at Graf or Lendl or McEnroe. None of them has truly classic form. But there are certain common characteristics to every good stroke, and you can use them as checkpoints to improve yours.

The basic assumption of self-correction is that there is something to correct. If your game is going great, you don't need to coach yourself. If you don't like the results you're getting, however, then you must correct the cause of those bad results.

Most players are unaware of what happens when they play. They hit the ball and they're either satisfied or frustrated with the result. They don't bother to analyze what has occurred. The problem is that most players, when practicing, only watch where the ball lands on the first bounce. The real secret to ball control, however, is where the ball lands on the second bounce, because that's the approximate spot, theoretically, where your opponent will be when he returns your shot. And ball control ultimately means control of your opponent.

THE SECOND-BOUNCE THEORY

The second-bounce theory is useful when practicing side-T shots, drop shots, and the serve. If you want to hit an effective ground stroke to a side-T, the second bounce should land outside the doubles alley because the purpose of a side-T shot should be to pull your opponent off the court.

On your drop shot, the second bounce, at worst, should land inside the service line, and ideally the ball should bounce three times inside the service box. The important thing on your drop-shot, however, is making the second bounce land as close as possible to the first bounce. This is accomplished with backspin (there is no such thing as a topspin dropshot). A good dropshot will clear the net by three to five feet. Anything higher will give your opponent too much time to get to the ball. And, if you hit the ball with too low an arc, the second bounce will probably land too deep in the court. If you're extremely close to the net, however, you can lower the arc.

The second-bounce theory is helpful on the serve too. For example, on a slice serve wide to the deuce court, the second bounce should land outside the doubles alley, and a topspin serve should hit the back fence *before* the second bounce.

THE FOUL-BALL THEORY: CORRECTING DIRECTION

The first point to remember is that there are only four basic errors in tennis: the ball goes too far to the right, too far to the left, too long, or too short (into the net).

The average player's conception of how to change the direction to the left or right (crosscourt or down the line) is to change the direction of his body and hit the ball exactly the same way—which is fine if he wants to let his opponent know where he's hitting the ball every time. Instead, the direction of the ball should be determined by whether you contact the ball early or late. This is the "foul-ball" theory. In baseball, if you're a right-handed batter and you hit the ball too late, the ball will go foul down the right-field line; if you hit the ball too early, it will go foul down the left-field line. And, just as in baseball, most players in tennis are "pull hitters." That is, they pull the ball crosscourt because it's very difficult to hit a ball late and control it.

Hitting early or late is directly related to the position of the foot closest to the net (the left foot—or right if you're left-handed—on the forehand). Ideally, to go crosscourt you should contact the ball in front of the lead foot. To go down the line, contact should occur even with or slightly behind the lead foot.

The direction of the ball is determined by the point of contact, not the body position, as many people believe. If you contact the ball behind your lead foot, it will go down the line. If you contact the ball in front of your lead foot, it will go crosscourt.

Tennis is an individual sport, however, and you have to experiment to discover what works best for you.

CORRECTING DISTANCE BY THE USE OF THE LEFT (OR NONRACQUET) HAND

The key to correcting short or long shots is the use of the left hand. The angle of the racquet face when it contacts the ball determines the vertical (up or down) direction the ball will take. If the racquet face is open, facing the sky, the ball naturally will go upward; if the face is closed, angling toward the ground, the ball will go downward. The angle of the racquet head can be adjusted through the use of the left hand. If you find yourself hitting long, close the racquet face a bit with your left hand. If you're hitting into the net, then open the racquet face with the left hand.

To correct your mistakes you must go through some trial and error as well as adjustment. If you make a mistake, don't hit two consecutive balls long or two consecutive balls short to correct the problem. Hit one long and one short by adjusting with the left hand until you zero in on the proper depth. Remember, every mistake in depth you make on your forehand or backhand is the fault of your left hand. So put your mind in your left hand.

Think left hand!

CHAPTER 8

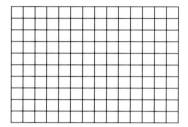

CHECKPOINTS FOR
THE GROUND STROKES

Many times a player will mishit a shot, then look down at his racquet as if to say, "How could you do this to me?" Once you begin to realize, however, what's actually happening when you mishit a shot, you can begin to correct the real cause of the trouble—you!

The fundamentals for both the forehand and the backhand are contact area, balance, and the use of the left hand. So when I teach ground strokes I seldom separate the forehand from the backhand. What you learn on the forehand you just flip over to the backhand side, because they're both ground strokes and the basic understanding of what to do is the same. You must hit everything—crosscourt shots, down-the-line shots, drop shots, lobs—from both sides. And if you have a problem on one side, you usually have it on the other as well. If you take too much of a backswing, you'll usually do it on both sides, and if you flip your wrist over on the forehand, you'll usually flip it over on the backhand as well. So the correction is often the same for the forehand and the backhand.

Before I go on to explain the checkpoints for ground strokes, I'd like to describe the different grips used by most players today. I want to emphasize first, however, that when a player is beginning to learn the game, I want them to use whatever grip is most natural for them *if* it does not present a medical problem.

First there is the *Eastern forehand* (the "shake-hands grip"). Put your palm flat against the strings and slide the palm down the shaft to the handle to get this grip.

Next is the *semi-Western forehand* (the "frying-pan grip"). Here the palm of the hand is farther under the racquet handle.

A way of obtaining the semi-Western grip is to first put the racquet flat on the ground and then pick it up.

And last there is the *Continental* (the "hammer grip"). The hand is on top of the racquet, and it is held just as if you were going to hammer a nail with the edge of the racquet.

WHY CHANGE GRIPS?

There's only one thing that significantly differs from backhand to forehand, and that's the grip. If you ask a hundred people why they change grips to hit a backhand, seventy-five will say their pro told them to do it and the other twenty-five will say they read it somewhere. They have virtually no real understanding of why they should change grips.

The reason you change from an Eastern or semi-Western forehand to a conventional Eastern or semi-Western backhand grip to hit a backhand is common sense—so you can have the ability to present the racquet face flat to the ball *and* have a firm wrist at the same time. If you don't change grips for a backhand and you try to present a flat racquet face to the ball, then your wrist will be contorted in some strange position. Or if you keep a firm wrist, the racquet face, with a forehand grip, will naturally be too open.

If you use a Continental grip for ground strokes, you do not need to change grips. But there are two serious disadvantages in using a Continental grip to hit, which is why I don't recommend it. First of all, to hit high-bouncing balls on your forehand, your arm is forced into a very awkward and weak position, making it difficult to generate power unless you've got extraordinary strength in your wrists. Second, on low-bouncing balls, in order to present the racquet face flat to the ball on the forehand, you must hit with a straight arm. And that's one of the easiest ways to develop tennis elbow.

THE SEMI-WESTERN FOREHAND

There has been a tremendous shift in the last ten to fifteen years among club and professional players alike to the semi-Western grip. The obvious advantage is that your arm and hand are in both the most comfortable and the most powerful position to hit the forehand with this grip.

Another advantage with the semi-Western forehand is that it allows you to hit the ball with the elbow tucked in closer to the body. This creates a very powerful and consistent shot. It's similar to a boxer throwing a punch with his elbows in close to his body for leverage and explosive power.

Take a look at Lendl's forehand. If you put boxing gloves on him, his fists would be moving similar to a pro boxer's. It's also true of a karate master. All his punches come with his elbows close to his body. That's where the power comes from.

The major problem with the semi-Western grip is that you can have problems with low balls because it's tough to get the racquet under the ball with that racquet-face position. It's also a little hard for some players to hit underspin with a semi-Western grip, so dropshots, lobs, and underspin approaches are more difficult for them to hit than with a Continental or Eastern grip.

LOOP- OR STRAIGHT-BACK PREPARATION?

There are two basic ways to prepare your racquet on the backswing—either with a loop or by simply bringing it straight back. With a loop backswing you bring the racquet back about shoulder height and gradually drop the racquet down to about the level of your waist (depending on the height of the ball you are about to hit) in a semicircular motion. The straight-back preparation is just that—the racquet, hand, and arm are taken straight back to hit the ball.

Both of these racquet preparations have advantages and disadvantages. I recommend, therefore, that you learn to use them both according to the match situation, the opponent, and the playing conditions.

The loop-back preparation, for example, can generate extra power, but it demands much better timing. So if you're mishitting a lot of balls go to a straight-back preparation.

The type of surface you're playing on is another one of the main factors that determines your racquet preparation. Basically, the faster the surface, the smaller your loop should be. Since you have less time to prepare, you don't have time to take a big loop on your backswing.

On a slower surface such as clay, you usually have plenty of time to set up for your shot and, also, the ball bounces higher. But since the ball is moving more slowly, you'll want to generate a bit more pace on the ball. A loop-back preparation is perfect for these situations.

The speed with which your opponent has hit the ball also determines your racquet preparation. If you're playing an opponent who hits softly, a loop backswing can help you hit with greater pace. If you're playing a big hitter a straight-back preparation is the ticket since you've got more time to get ready for

your shot with this simple backswing. Also, since your opponent is supplying most of the power, a short compact swing is all you need to hit the ball hard. Of course, if you're playing an opponent who can hit the ball at all speeds, it's best if you can use both preparations so you'll be able to cope with whatever he hits at you.

As the match wears on the balls will usually fluff up and become heavier. On clay courts it's even more pronounced. As the balls pick up clay they feel like a heavy stone. With the balls slowed down, a loop backswing again can help you add power as you need it.

There are three common denominators among the top forehands in the world today: the racquet face is closed, the elbow is bent and kept close to the body, and the lower part of the body is well balanced throughout the swing even if the player leaves his feet to hit the ball.

There are two basic ways to prepare your racquet. You can use a loop-back or a straight-back preparation. The loop is generally used on slower surfaces or when you have more time. The straight-back preparation is preferred on faster surfaces or against harder-hit balls.

If you like to hit the ball early and you're playing an opponent who hits high, arcing shots, use a simple preparation. If you like to take or contact the ball low, two to four feet behind the baseline like Borg used to do, then like Björn you can use a loop backswing to generate more pace.

The weather is also important. On a hot day the ball tends to move through the air faster, so a quicker setup is preferable. On a humid day the heavy air will slow the ball down, so use the loop for power. On a windy day when the ball is being blown all over the place, fouling up your timing, a straight backswing is much easier to time.

OPEN OR CLOSED STANCE?

Many teaching pros will insist that you turn sideways to hit the ball. But more and more the open-stance forehand is becoming popular in tennis today. And that's an important step because being able to hit an open-stance forehand gives you some added advantages.

A closed-stance forehand.

In an open-stance fore-
hand, the weight of the
body is predominantly on
the right foot.

The major objection to open-stance ground strokes goes
something like this: "You don't transfer your weight into the
ball if you don't step over and into it. You just arm the ball."

But the truth is an open-stance forehand provides a balanced
and stable foundation for your shot. (Besides, the weight transfer
even in a closed-stance shot occurs before the player hits the
ball. So if you're balanced it doesn't matter which foot you hit
off of.) The difference is that you hit off your back foot with
an open stance and off your front foot with a closed stance. And
that's where the objection comes in. If you hit off your back
foot with a closed stance, your weight is actually falling backward, off balance, and away from the shot, and you'll often hit
a weak, short shot. But that doesn't apply to an open-stance
forehand. The back foot is the source of balance in an open
stance. If the back knee is bent the body should be in balance.
The ball doesn't know if you're hitting off your front or back
foot. It reacts to the way it's hit. And if its struck with a solid,
balanced body, it will come off the racquet face with power.

The myth that you "arm" the ball, that you don't get your
body into the shot with an open stance and, therefore, you lose
power, is just that—a myth. Tests conducted with a radar speed

63

gun show a slight and unimportant loss of two to four miles per hour with an open stance. And some players, myself included, actually hit the ball harder because they're comfortable hitting the ball that way.

What are the advantages of the open-stance forehand (and backhand, for that matter)? If you don't have to bring your front foot around to hit the ball, that's one less step you have to take. That means you can cover a lot more court.

Also, your recovery time is much quicker with an open-stance shot. You're already facing the court when you hit the shot. With a closed stance you must bring your lead foot back to the middle to start your run to the next shot. But with an open stance you simply push off your outside foot and you're on your way. This means you will save two steps on every shot—one after you've hit the ball and one when you get to the next shot in order to close your stance again. Since a player takes an average of three steps to get to his opponent's next shot in a typical match, it means a player who hits exclusively closed-stance ground strokes must run nearly twice as far as his open-stance opponent.

The biggest advantage of the open stance, however, is when you're returning a serve. When you're playing someone with a big serve, you barely have time to move your racquet into place to block the ball, much less go through a lot of foot movement. And if you can only hit from a closed stance, you will rarely have time to set up for a decent return.

Although an open-stance backhand is rarely used in a rally, it's ideal for returning a serve. The open stance allows you to return balls hit directly at you that would normally jam you if you tried to step over to close your stance. Also, the hard-hit serve and the wide serve are a lot easier to get back with the added quickness and reach of the open stance.

CHECKPOINTS FOR GROUND STROKES

The principal checkpoints for any ground stroke are, of course, the fundamentals of good stroking: contact area, balance, and the use of the left (or nonracquet) hand.

CORRECTING THE CONTACT AREA

Perhaps the major problem most players develop on their ground strokes is the overworking of the racquet head. The racquet head seems to be flying all over the place—whipping over the shoulder, slapping at the ball, flopping all around in the backswing. To check this problem:

For a good backhand you should prepare the racquet with the arms bent, maintain good balance with the lower part of the body, and keep the racquet head going through the ball without having the upper part of the body turn too much.

1. Think "fast feet, slow arm." Pretend your arm is in slow motion and concentrate on a fluid, controlled swing.

2. Squeeze tightly with the last three fingers on your racquet hand as you hit. This creates a firm wrist and eliminates the slapping motion of the racquet.

3. Freeze at the end of the stroke to check your finish. Can you see the racquet between you and the ball, or has it wrapped back around your shoulder?

In the past coaches insisted that both feet remain planted on ground strokes, but many players today are jumping when they hit the ball and their left foot is landing two to three feet beyond the point of contact. Steffi Graf is a master of this shot.

With the heavy topspin shots being hit at them, it is often essential for the players to leave the ground in order to get on top of these high-bouncing balls. This enables them to gain the leverage necessary to handle these powerful shots. But remember to keep your balance throughout the shot so when you land you don't have to take a step or two to recover for the next shot.

4. When you hit, think "palm forward" on the forehand and "knuckles forward" on the backhand. This helps increase your awareness of contact area.

5. Get a visual image of hitting through four balls. I often have students take a racquet without strings and swing through four balls "strung" together on a coat hanger so they can get a mental picture of hitting through the ball.

CORRECTING BALANCE

After you hit, freeze and see if you can place your racquet on the ground between your feet. This will indicate if your feet are properly spaced, and by forcing yourself to stop, you can check any unnecessary use of recovery steps.

CHECKING FOR THE USE OF THE LEFT HAND

In practice, wipe your racquet hand on your shorts between each shot to ensure that the racquet is in the left hand. Remember, all mistakes on the ground strokes are the fault of the left hand. Think left hand!

CHAPTER 9

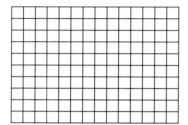

MANAGING YOUR VOLLEY

THE MYTHS ABOUT THE VOLLEY

There are some common phrases used in connection with the volley that I believe can be too easily misinterpreted. One of them is "punching the volley" and the other is "hitting the ball as far out in front of you as possible."

Many people's conception of a punch involves straightening the arm, and doing this on the forehand volley is, I believe, the single most detrimental movement when hitting this stroke. An effective forehand volley covers only a distance of six to ten inches. It is hit with your arm starting bent and finishing bent. You want minimal racquet motion on the volley, and on a punch the racquet motion is often too long. Additionally, the player who tries to contact the ball too far in front of him, who straightens his arm prematurely, will be unable to adjust to anything unexpected—wind, opponent's mishits, or his own miscalculations. More importantly, he loses his potential for power because he loses the potential to accelerate through the ball.

Another widespread misconception is that you should change your grip back and forth for backhand and forehand volleys. There is seldom time for such adjustments on a normally paced ball hit from the baseline or when two players are at the net volleying at close range, which often happens in doubles.

USE A CONTINENTAL GRIP FOR VOLLEYS

One of the few things I will insist on in this book is that if you want a sound volley, it must be hit with a Continental grip. The Continental grip is the only grip that enables you (on both

One of the greatest failures of today's coaches is allowing their students, particularly young girls, to use two hands to hit their backhand volley. Not only will the two-handed backhand volley limit their reach, but it never allows the player to develop the necessary muscle structure in her forearms to someday hit a decent backhand volley.

backhand and forehand) to simultaneously have a firm wrist and an open racquet face—the two key elements for a good volley.

Without the Continental grip you will never develop the proper feel or accomplish what you want to do with the volley. You can hit a forehand over with almost any grip. You can hit a backhand over with almost any grip. But you can't volley adequately with any grip. It's the way the body is built.

That's the reason you see so many players today who can't volley. The problem with hitting so many power ground strokes from the baseline is that the player never learns how to hit a volley. In the first place the forehand volley is probably the toughest shot in tennis, and the power ground-strokers with semi-Western grips find the touch necessary for this shot very difficult to acquire *unless* they were taught right from the beginning to volley with a Continental grip. The two-handed player also has trouble volleying because he never develops the muscles or the feel to hit a one-handed backhand volley. And a two-handed backhand volley is severely limiting. Of course, if you hit with a semi-Western forehand and a two-handed backhand, you've got double the problem.

One of the most damaging things a coach can do is not to teach a player a one-handed backhand volley. If he allows his students, especially juniors, to hold on to the racquet with both hands when hitting the backhand volley, he's automatically killing their future as a net player.

Chris Evert, as hard as she has tried, has never learned to volley to her potential. Even her coach, Dennis Ralston, who I rate as one of the top three volleyers in the history of the game, couldn't teach her to volley. All because Chris stayed with a two-handed backhand volley for too long.

There has seldom been a good two-handed volleyer throughout the history of the game. The touch and reach problems of a two-handed volley can never be overcome. The best ever probably was Jimmy Connors, and you could never put Connors into the same company with even an average net player. Anything wide and low to Jimmy's backhand volley was very difficult for him to handle. The reason Connors was effective at the net at all was because he chose the right ball to approach on and he hit great approaches. If he hit a poor approach or was forced to come to the net, Jimmy was very vulnerable.

COURT POSITIONING ON VOLLEYS

Volleys should only be hit from three places on the court:

1. The "ideal volley position," or IVP, is halfway between the net and the service line. It is ideal because you can get back

and cover a lob from that position and yet still prevent the opponent from getting the ball down at your feet.

2. The "defensive volley position," or DVP, is around the service line. When hitting a volley the only difference between an IVP and DVP volley is the length of the contact area, *not the length of the backswing.* That's where most players make their mistake. You must penetrate through the ball farther (in other words, extend your contact area), not take a bigger backswing.

The only time you should hit a volley from the DVP is on the first volley when serving and volleying. You don't go for winners from here because you're usually not in a position to hit side-T angles, which means it's too difficult to put the ball away. Also, the greater distance to your opponent's baseline allows him plenty of time to get to the ball. To go for the side T at the wrong time or for a deep winning volley from the DVP is dumb tennis. The idea is to get yourself into position to hit a put-away volley by setting your opponent up.

3. The "easiest volley position," or EVP, is right on top of the net. You should only volley this close to the net if the ball is a setup and you can move up there and put it away. If you station yourself in the EVP as a matter of course, a smart opponent will lob on every shot, since you're completely vulnerable to even a mediocre lob by being way too close to the net. Only a weak or nonthinking opponent will hit to you when you're in the EVP.

SERVE AND VOLLEY—THE CHECK STEP

The check step is a little hop you take to check your forward run to the net. The idea is to land on the balls of your feet with your head over your belly button in perfect balance so you are ready to go in any direction the ball is hit.

If you forget the check step all your opponent has to do is hit the ball wide and you're dead. You'll never be able to stop your forward momentum in time to change direction and get to the ball. But if you're taking a good check step almost no one can pass you outright.

The difficulty in the check step is not in knowing how to do it but *when* to do it. Timing is critical. The check step should occur *just prior* to your opponent contacting the ball. In other words, you should get in as close as you can *before* your opponent hits the ball.

Very few people really know how or when to take a check step. The ball hits their opponent's racquet and they are still running forward. They do not check their forward movement in time. This is because most players think that they've got to get to the service line to make their first volley. Getting to the service line is their sole objective, not timing the check step to coincide with the moment just before the opponent touches the ball. The good serve-and-volleyers have a perfectly timed check step.

Another reason for a poor check step is bad balance. Your upper body may be too far in front of your lower body when coming in. That will throw it out of balance and you won't be able to check your forward movement. It can also come from being overweight or your legs not being strong enough.

To check your balance during a practice session, slip a racquet handle in the back of your pants. As you come in to volley the racquet head must stay in contact with both shoulder blades. This forces you to keep your back straight as you come in so you maintain your center of gravity and your balance.

One major mistake many players make after taking their check step is they only think of moving left or right. They don't continue forward as well. They move laterally to get to a wide shot instead of diagonally forward to meet it as close to the net as possible. The purpose of the check step is only to determine the direction of your opponent's return of serve. Once you've determined that, you continue to move forward either straight ahead or diagonally. You keep closing to the IVP.

To practice check steps, serve to your practice partner and instead of returning your serve have him catch it and see if you have taken your check step properly *and* in time.

There are occasions when you eliminate the check step altogether. If a player runs through his check step he can get closer to the net for his first volley. And that can be a devastating shot. McEnroe often eliminates the check step, especially on forcing serves. When he was at his peak he didn't need to check step because his serve was so great. That made him all the more lethal because he was making most of his first volleys at the IVP instead of the DVP. And from the IVP he could go right for a winner. The opponent never even got a chance to pass him.

But eliminating the check step is also a very risky play. If the opponent returns the ball anywhere but down the middle, you probably won't be able to recover in time to get to the ball. So you eliminate the check step when you are pretty sure your opponent will return your serve down the middle.

One final point about the serve and volley. You must make up your mind *before* you serve whether you intend to serve and volley. That's why club players often appear slower than the tournament players when coming in behind their serve. The club player tends to wait to see how he served and then he decides whether to come in or not. By then it's too late. The good tournament player has made up his mind to come in *before* he tosses the ball up to serve. After that he never hesitates.

73

MANAGING YOUR VOLLEY

CHECKPOINTS FOR THE VOLLEY

RACQUET FACE OPEN

When volleying, your racquet face should almost always be open. The only exception is when you're volleying away an easy setup close to the net. The Continental grip allows you to have both a firm wrist and an open racquet face. Why do you want an open racquet face? To create backspin. Why do you want backspin? Because it's your control spin, and the volley, contrary to popular belief, is not a big slam-bang shot. It is a control shot.

If you want to develop control of your volley, develop backspin. Spin causes friction as the ball travels through the air. More spin causes more friction, and that causes the ball to drop into the court sooner. That is the basic principle for controlling depth. Also, an open racquet face is critical when hitting low volleys. The volley cannot be a straight-line shot if the ball is hit from anywhere below the top of the net. If the ball is low you must be able to put arc on the ball in order to clear the net.

To hit deep, use less spin; to hit short, use more spin. This is a very simple approach, and though hitting backspin on your volleys is sometimes a difficult concept to learn initially, like anything else, as you learn the feel of it you learn to adjust, adding a bit more or less spin to get the result you desire. I want you to think of the *long term*, so stick with it. There's a future in this concept.

The only other way to adjust the depth on your volleys is to hit either harder or softer, which is a very unpredictable method. The advantage of spin as opposed to speed is that the speed with which you can hit the ball differs every day because of many reasons, including your biorhythms (some days you come out feeling fantastic and you can really pound the ball) different altitudes, and different balls. Trying to adjust distance by how hard you hit the ball is just not always practical. Whether you like it or not, the speed of the ball will change from day to day, but spin is your old reliable. Once you master the technique you can add or reduce spin consciously without other factors affecting the result.

A flat volleyer can never consistently hit the side-T volley because he can't control the depth of the shot. It's only good when he's tight to the net. This is the reason there are so few good forehand volleys.

Whenever the ball is hit directly at you on a volley, you should throw your elbow out to the side rather than try to jump out of the way and take it on your forehand.

Volleys should be hit with an open racquet face, which will give your volley natural backspin. Although you can get away with hitting the ball flat on high volleys, backspin is absolutely essential on low volleys. If you do not open your racquet face, the ball has little chance of going over the net on a low volley.

Even though you may be in difficulty at the net on a wide ball, it's important that you strive to keep the racquet face open. This will enable you to keep your volley under control even though your body is not.

The good volleyers like Pat Cash all have good feel. Contrary to popular belief you develop feel by developing backspin. See, backspin is your control spin and feel is the ultimate control. You would never say a player who blasts topspin off both sides is a feel player. It's always the control shots that denote a player with touch or feel. Most touch shots are hit with backspin. So if you develop a backspin volley, you will develop feel and you will be a good volleyer.

THINK "CATCH"

In order to learn backspin you must learn to get under the ball. That's why I teach the volley as a catch. If you want to catch a ball you don't slap at it, you get under it. Thinking "catch" enables you to remember to maintain an open racquet face while volleying. Usually if your volley falls apart, you'll start dumping the ball into the net. If you think catch it will help you to get under the ball, put a good arc on it, and get it over the net.

Think catch!

A valuable tip if your volley starts to stray—hit a couple of drop volleys and it will usually return immediately. The key to the game is to always have a foundation you can go back to when things go wrong. The foundation for the volley is the concept of catch, which is the essence of the drop volley.

Everybody thinks the drop volley is the most advanced volley. Actually, you build your volley from the drop volley. I teach a drop volley first and have the student hit the ball gradually deeper and deeper. When you catch the ball it will just bounce off your strings. If you then put a little extra backspin on the ball, that's a drop volley. Simply extend the contact area, and you've got your deep volley back.

Once a player can hit a true backspin drop volley, you know he's hitting with underspin and he's got the understanding of the volley.

A good way to start learning the volley is to simply practice catching a ball without a racquet. Then try using a ''catching'' racquet to develop a natural feel for the short catching motion of the volley. After that, use a racquet with strings and think ''catch'' as you volley.

The ball will always go exactly where your strings are pointing. In other words, if you present the racquet face in a certain direction, the ball will always go there. If the wrist and racquet head are both parallel to the net at point of contact, the ball will go directly back across the net, which is to say, down the line. If the racquet head is slightly ahead of the wrist, the ball will go crosscourt. It's that simple. So to correct problems of direction on the volley, use the checkpoint "wrist and racquet head together" and watch where your racquet strings are pointing after you hit the ball. (*Note*: Direction is not so easily calculated on ground strokes because to hit down the line you must contact the ball behind your lead foot, but volleys are usually hit a little in front no matter what their direction. This one small difference is critical.) The successful volleyers in professional tennis direct their volleys rather than power them.

The player who lets his racquet head get ahead of his wrist will usually volley the ball down the center when he wants to go down the line. This is a critical bit of misdirection because generally when you're in trouble you should volley down the line. A crosscourt volley (unless you can hit an outright winner) opens up the entire court for your opponent to hit into, and to properly cover the court you will have to shift to the opposite side of the center line to cut down your opponent's angles. If you're in trouble you usually don't have time for such adjustments, which means you're wide open for even mediocre passing shots.

MAINTAIN A FIRM WRIST

If you don't maintain a firm wrist on your volleys, a hard-hit ball will often force the racquet face to pop open, which will cause the ball to pop up. Or the racquet will sometimes turn in your hand. This gives players, especially women, the feeling that the ball is stronger than they are because they can't hold on to the racquet, which in turn helps create the fear that so many players have at the net. It's a definite psychological blow when someone knocks your racquet loose. You begin to think, Geez, I've got no business at the net.

To firm up the wrist, squeeze the bottom three fingers of the racquet hand.

KEEP THE RACQUET HEAD UP

This is especially helpful if your volleys are falling short. If your racquet head is up, you'll have a firmer wrist and you'll tend to play the ball higher than normal. Anytime you can play the ball higher it increases your chances of getting the ball over the net, and if you drop your racquet head you will inevitably hit the ball at a lower position. This often means the difference between taking the ball above or below the level of the net. With this simple adjustment, you will have gone from a defensive to an offensive position. And that's often the difference between winning and losing.

MINIMIZE THE BACKSWING AND FOLLOW-THROUGH

What is the purpose of the backswing? To add power, of course. But that is not necessary when volleying. The volley is a controlled directional shot. If you follow through, the racquet head flies ahead of your wrist and you decrease your potential to go down the line.

KEEP THE VOLLEY COMPACT

The great volleyers are compact volleyers like Pat Cash and John McEnroe. But all their strokes, not just the volley, are compact. On the other hand Ivan Lendl, who has big body turns on his ground strokes and a big windup, is not a strong volleyer even though he has painstakingly tried to improve his net game. The lesson, then, is to shorten your stroke and try to hit the ball as close to you as possible.

If you stretch too far out front or to the side, your arm will be prematurely straightened prior to contact. This means you've eliminated any potential for necessary adjustments due to wind or strange spins. Most important, you have eliminated the potential to lengthen your contact area and to accelerate within the contact area, which enables you to increase your power without taking a bigger swing. See, different volleys have different contact areas. On a DVP volley, a volley taken around the service line, you need to lengthen the contact area because the ball must travel a greater distance to land at the opponent's baseline than on a normal volley taken at the net. Whereas on a ball hit very hard directly at you when you're right on top of the net, you need only a minimal contact area—just block the ball.

KEEP A TWO-BALL SPACE BETWEEN YOUR ELBOW AND STOMACH

This is particularly important for forehand volleys because the tendency is to let the right elbow get behind the right hip, in which case the stroke gets cramped and your power zone is eliminated.

Players who learn "racquet back" to hit ground strokes tend to do the same when they come to the net to hit the volley. Consequently, they also take a big swing at their volleys. A good volley, however, should have little or no backswing and virtually no follow-through.

When reaching wide for a
volley a player should use
a "crossover" step. If you
move your outside foot toward the ball it severely
limits your reach. But by
using the crossover, a
player can add at least an
additional racquet length
to his reach.

82

KEEP A BENT ARM (ON FOREHAND VOLLEYS)

A good forehand volley is only a six- to ten-inch stroke, depending on the length of your arm and other variables. If you straighten your arm in a punching motion, you're doing too much—the potential for mishits and misdirection increases as the length of your swing increases.

TURN SIDEWAYS

Turning sideways when volleying is related to the so-called crossover or cross-in step. When a player crosses his left foot over his right foot on a forehand volley (right to left on the backhand) it increases his reach by one full racquet length.

On the forehand volley the elbow should start bent and finish bent. But on the backhand volley the arm should start bent and finish straight.

PLAY DOUBLES FOR A BETTER VOLLEY

One final tip about volleying: if you want to develop a good volley, play more doubles. A good doubles player gets to the net as much as possible, and that means he hits a lot of volleys and learns the special touch and feel required to be good up at the net.

Mats Wilander is a perfect example of a player who has benefited from playing doubles. He has become a much better volleyer because he usually plays both singles and doubles in tournaments. In fact, his volley was the key ingredient in his thrilling five-set victory over Ivan Lendl in the 1988 U.S. Open. Playing doubles is part of the Swedish team mentality. The entire team—from Wimbledon-champ Stefan Edberg to Anders Jarryd to Wilander—all play doubles together. As a consequence, unlike other Europeans who grew up on clay courts, most of the Swedes are excellent volleyers.

MANAGING YOUR HALF VOLLEY

Nobody enjoys a half volley. If you gave a good player an option, he'd probably rather hit any other shot. That's the one shot that really bothers a player. So that's the shot you try to make your opponent hit a lot.

The mechanics of a good half volley are simple to explain. No backswing and no follow-through. For a half volley it's the simpler the better. The less you do, the better off you'll be.

Another important point when hitting a half volley is that you should prepare your racquet face so it's perpendicular to the ground at contact. You don't half-volley with an open racquet face, as on a regular volley. That creates backspin and the ball will tend to pop up, thereby giving your opponent an easy chance at a passing shot. The half volley should be hit with either slight topspin or flat. So keep the racquet face perpendicular to the court. If you close the racquet face you'll end up with a short ball or a ball hit into the net.

There is one exception, however. If you keep a flat or open racquet face on a half volley against an extremely heavy topspin shot, the ball will tend to fly off your racquet. The basic principle in this case is "counter spin with spin." So close the racquet face a little (that is, put some topspin on your half volley) on hard topspin balls.

Over the years there have been very few players who could hit the half volley well consistently. Most players just scoop it back. It's usually a soft, midcourt return or they pop it up for an easy putaway for their opponent. The good players keep it deep.

With a volley, the ball should be hit with an open racquet face, but the key to hitting the half volley is to make sure that your racquet face is flat, or perpendicular to the ground. If the half volley is hit with an open racquet face, the ball will pop up.

Players also make a lot of mistakes with a half volley because they try to hit a winner off it from a defensive position. Or they will try to hit a full-out ground stroke—maybe crosscourt to a side T—a very difficult shot that most of the time doesn't work.

CHAPTER 10

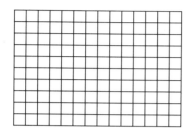

MANAGING YOUR SERVE AND OVERHEAD

YOU'RE ONLY AS GOOD AS YOUR SECOND SERVE

The second serve is the foundation of your service game, not the first serve. If you don't have a solid, reliable second serve, your first serve will be of minimal value.

Would you rather buy a car that goes one hundred miles per hour and has lousy brakes or one that goes fifty and has great brakes? Then why do so many players pound their first serve as fast as possible and then dink the second one in? Remember, you're only as good a player as your second serve. That statement may hurt, but it's true. You've got to develop a dependable and penetrating second serve.

The major differences in today's game over the game of thirty years ago are the tremedous power of the service return and the penetration of the second serve. Today's players hit their second serve much harder. They've been forced to because of the way their opponents are hitting their returns. You can no longer just kick it in and come in and make a good volley. The returner just won't let you do it. He'll kill any ball that's just sitting up there.

The new era of returning has forced an improvement in the second serve. A good second serve has depth and penetration. It's a shot your opponent cannot exploit to put you in trouble. A really great second serve is a shot that means you are still in charge. Which means you are in a position to hit a forcing volley or a penetrating ground stroke off the return.

Spend a lot of time developing your second serve. Until you get a dependable and penetrating second serve, forget the first serve. Besides, your first serve should be a more powerful version of your second serve, not the reverse.

The smart servers identify quickly when their first serve is not on and they then concentrate on accelerating their second serve and using that for their first delivery. If you have good mechanics on your second serve, you can beef it up and use it as a first serve.

Mats Wilander is a very smart server. Once he gets into a pattern where his first serve is not going in, he concentrates on hitting a three-quarter-speed first serve or a hard-hit second serve. It's not as powerful as his first serve, but it has enough spin and bite to keep his opponent off balance. And that's important because you seldom see a guy at any level successfully attacking the first serve and coming in. It's too dangerous. The server can slug a powerful first serve at any time, and if the opponent is caught chipping and charging the net, he's usually dead.

Another important point—what's the difference in racquet speed between the first and second serve? That's easy. There isn't any.

It is very important to remember not to drastically alter your arm speed when hitting a second serve. That leads not only to inaccuracy and double faults, but also to choking. When you're under extreme pressure to get the ball in, like on a second serve at 30–40, you'll tend to baby the ball with a slow swing. The natural motion of your arm will be impeded, and you'll freeze up. The second serve should be hit with the same effort and power as the first. Only the server's energy is directed into adding more spin to the ball.

Your second serve is not just a slower version of your first serve, because that implies you're depending on gravity to make the ball fall into the service box. And the use of gravity is a beginner's technique. Instead, use spin. Spin slows the ball down by creating friction with the air, and you can control spin under pressure more easily than you can control speed. With spin you can maintain the same service rhythm and the same arm speed on every serve, yet still slow the ball down and make it drop into the service box when you need it most.

The energy of the first serve should be directed mostly into hitting the ball forward. In other words, getting as much speed on the ball as possible and still getting it in. So that means less spin, less arc on the ball, less clearance of the net—and more speed and power. But it also means less accuracy and a lower percentage of balls hit in. The more spin, arc, and clearance of the net on your serve, the higher your percentages will be. That means you can raise your percentages not by swinging more slowly, but by imparting more spin to the ball. It's that simple.

You want to hit the ball harder? Hit it with less spin. You want your percentages to go up? Serve with more spin.

You should also adjust your serve according to how your opponent likes to hit his returns. First, determine the length of his backswing by the distance he takes the racquet away from his body. If he takes the racquet back wide, serve into him or at him; if he has a compact swing, serve wide. Second, notice what types of spin your opponent can hit. If he can only hit backspin on the backhand side, then you should concentrate on moving into the net because he will tend to float the ball or chip it short. Third, hit a high-kicking serve against a two-hander because most players are not as comfortable reaching up. (The most effective serve, however, against a two-hander is a lefty's slice serve because the ball slides away from his already-limited reach.) Fourth, against someone who runs around his backhand to take the ball on his forehand side, or against someone who attacks your serve and comes in, hit a slice serve because the ball will move away from him.

This presumes that you can hit a slice, topspin, and flat serve. If you can't, your game is limited to what you can do. My strong recommendation is that you begin immediately to develop the three basic serves. Go out and practice until you can hit these serves and then test them in match play. If you don't, you'll definitely be limited.

THE THREE BASIC SERVES AND THE CLOCK THEORY

A good server thinks like a good baseball pitcher. He doesn't just rear back and throw it as hard as he can. A smart pitcher has a variety of pitches and speeds with which he can keep the batter off balance.

It's the same way with a good server. He doesn't just have one serve and one speed. He's got an arsenal of serves to throw at his opponent. There are three basic serves that a player can develop. They are the slice serve, the topspin serve, and the flat serve. By far the most important of these is the topspin.

The best way to explain and to learn how to hit each of the three basic serves is through the "clock theory." Each of the three serves is struck by the racquet face at a different place on the ball. So if you imagine that the tennis ball is the face of a clock, you can easily identify where each serve is struck.

The slice serve is struck somewhere between two and three o'clock (for a right-handed server). The problem with a slice serve is you are not hitting as far under the ball as on a topspin serve, which is the principal action that makes the ball go up over the net. (The topspin on the ball drags it back down into the court.) So your margin of error is lowered somewhat on a slice serve. It is simply a tougher serve to get into your opponent's service box. It often goes wide or into the net.

If you're hitting a slice serve and it's constantly going wide, turn your body to the side so your back is almost to the net (like John McEnroe) and then serve. Your ball will immediately go down the middle. Then slowly turn back around until the slice is going where you want it to. Gradually, you will move the serve over and soon you will be taking a normal service stance and hitting the slice serve in.

The topspin serve is struck at about seven o'clock with the racquet face going up over the top of the ball, somewhere around two o'clock. This causes the ball to rotate almost directly upward over itself from around seven o'clock to two o'clock. The topspin serve allows the server to hit the ball hard, and yet the spin on the ball drags the ball down into the court. The ball also has a tendency to bounce very high to a right-hander's backhand. And that's a tough shot for most players. The topspin serve, therefore, is very effective as a second serve and to mix up your first serve and keep your opponent guessing.

But probably most important of all, the topspin serve has a great clearance of the net, which cuts down on the potential for errors by at least 75 percent. So a player hitting a good topspin serve has less tendency to choke. You get good clearance of the net, which automatically gives you penetration and height on the ball, two very important factors in a good second serve.

The best way I've ever found to teach a topspin serve is for the student to stand outside the court and try to hit the ball over the fence into the far service box. In order to hit a topspin serve you've got to learn to get under the ball and hit up, and it's impossible to clear the fence unless you do.

Do not confuse the topspin serve with the American twist serve, however. I do not recommend that anyone learn to hit the twist serve, even though it is a highly effective shot. The twist is very unpredictable and difficult for a returner to get any rhythm on. It jumps high and has a vicious bite when it hits the ground, so it literally explodes off the court. But medically the twist serve is a very dangerous stroke. Players in the past who used it extensively almost to a man developed very painful and debilitating back problems that lasted a lifetime.

The toss creates the twist serve—and its problems. You hit it around the same place on the ball as the topspin serve, at about seven o'clock, with a swing upward toward two o'clock. But for the kick you throw the ball farther behind your head, which means you must bend your back way over, putting a tremendous strain on the vertebrae and muscles of the back.

The last of the three basic serves, and the least important (except for world-class players), is the flat serve. The flat serve is the most powerful serve. It's hit with a flat racquet face directly in the middle of the clock, so the ball has very little spin on it —it's flat. It travels very quickly, but it has no spin to slow it up or drag it down into the court. There is very little margin for error on this serve, and so its usefulness is very limited.

The flat serve is good to throw in as a change of pace, when you're up 40–0 or you're going for an ace. But for most players it should be used only when you're confident and getting a high percentage in. Oddly, many club players, especially the young athletic males, use it as their number-one serve. They blast that baby in there and they can really hit it too. They get six, eight, ten aces a set with it sometimes. The problem is, it rarely goes in and they're left hitting second serve after second serve. That leads to lots of double faults and weak, easily attacked second serves.

My advice is to stay strictly away from a flat serve until you have developed good dependable topspin and slice serves. The flat serve is just the final icing on a very well-rounded service game. It's not the main course.

USE THE CONTINENTAL GRIP

If you want to develop the three basic serves and have a strong and dependable service game, the Continental grip is essential. Now if you're sixty years old and you're comfortable with an Eastern forehand grip and you don't want to go through the aggravation of the change, fine, stick with your old grip. But if you hate your serve and you want to change, then the Continental is the way to go.

If you're a young player coming up, you must change to a Continental or face a frustrating future. The Continental grip is uncomfortable at first for most players, but what new technique isn't? Stick with it. All other grips severely limit your future as a tennis player.

CHECKPOINTS FOR THE SERVE

THINK "WRIST" ON THE SERVE

Most pros teach that the toss is the most important part of the serve. They have their students practice tossing the ball so that it will land in a chalk-marked area just in front of them or do some other drill to achieve the perfect toss. This is nonsense, because there are four times when the perfect toss won't be possible:

1. If you toss the ball to your regular height on a windy day, it will blow off course. The toss, therefore, must be lower.

2. When the sun is in your favorite toss spot, you must alter the toss to one side or the other to avoid blinding yourself.

3. When you're in a pressure situation—it's match point against you or you're playing mixed doubles and you've just served two double faults in a row and your partner is wondering whether you'll ever get it in—jumpy nerves will alter your toss.

4. The tossing hand is often uncoordinated. If you're right-handed and you throw a ball left-handed, you know how ridiculous you can look. The toss is just as difficult a chore for the left hand to perform, and therefore you probably won't always get a dependable toss.

Instead of concentrating on the toss, concentrate on your wrist. The wrist is critical because it makes the serve go wherever it goes—left, right, long, or short. Hitting the ball short or long is related to hitting up or snapping down with the wrist. Hitting left or right is caused by rotating the wrist to the left or right. If the ball is going into the net, think "hit up." If the ball is going long, think "snap down."

Even a baseball pitcher primarily uses his wrist to control the ball and to give it the real snap in his throw. That's why I have my students throw a ball to learn the serve. This forces them to learn to use the wrist. It's exactly like a pitcher throwing a pitch—curves and fastballs both require a wrist snap.

A couple of well-known coaches are espousing the theory that the wrist should be locked on every shot—even on the serve. They've got slow-motion film showing the wrist at impact. The problem is it's all wrong. The locked-wrist theory is destroying many a tennis player's future. Not only does it limit the possibilities of your serve, but it leads to injury.

Once you lock your wrist all the muscles in your forearm contract and the part of your arm that takes the force is the elbow. What follows is tennis elbow.

Beyond that, the serve should be a whiplike action, and no one can move only their shoulder and generate enough speed to produce any power on the ball. The end of any whip snaps when you've used it properly. And what's at the end of your own personal whip, your arm? Why, your wrist, of course, ready and waiting to be snapped. Snap your wrist for power and control —and to prevent injury! It's that simple.

Another important point if you want to get that whip into

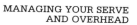

If you want to improve your serve, try to copy the throwing motion of a baseball player. If you have a natural throwing motion, your hand will come from behind your head. But in order to throw the ball accurately, you will have to keep a loose wrist.

Most women will naturally throw sidearm. This motion makes it very difficult for them to think about "scratching the back" on the serve, but is all right as long as the wrist is kept loose.

your serve is to relax completely. Is every muscle in your upper body completely relaxed before you start your service motion? When it is, begin your serve. That's why you'll often see a pro shake out his arms before he serves. He's trying to get his muscles relaxed.

That's the thing about a whip—it's very loose. And that looseness causes the snapping motion at the end that supplies the real sting. It's also what gives the sting to your serve.

When you accelerate your wrist through the ball, you add a tremendous amount of power and pace to your ground strokes, especially the forehand. And it's the same with the serve.

Also, the clock theory won't work unless you have a loose wrist on the serve. If you're going to hit your slice serve at three o'clock, you have to be able to come around the ball. And you have to be able to hit up into your serve to hit topspin. These all require a completely flexible wrist.

To avoid a locked-wrist serve do not put the ball against the strings of the racquet as you prepare to serve. That leads automatically to a locked wrist because the racquet hand is forced to support the racquet while waiting to serve. Instead, have the racquet rest on the bottom three free fingers of the tossing hand.

The best servers in the world keep their bottom three fingers completely loose. Some players even take the bottom two or three fingers off the racquet while serving to ensure a loose-wristed motion.

A locked wrist limits a server's ability to hit different types of serves as well as control the ball. Starting your serve with the ball placed against the strings of the racquet forces you to maintain a locked wrist in order to keep the racquet head up. Players who hold their racquet out in front of them almost as if they were carrying a flag also have a locked wrist.

Some servers, such as John McEnroe, actually start with the racquet head pointing to the ground. This helps ensure that their wrist will be completely relaxed before they start serving.

STAY BALANCED THROUGHOUT THE SERVE

A study was done of players at all levels, from beginners to touring pros, in which they served with their feet immobilized so all they could do was use their arms to serve. It was found that the pros could hit the ball from 90 to 95 percent as fast using only their arms. The club players retained almost 100 percent of their speed, and many actually hit the ball harder without an elaborate windup.

So all that fancy body movement, all that stylish hip waggle and back arch and big grunt, is superfluous to a good serve. It's all in the wrist—how you move the wrist to control the spin and how you snap the wrist for power.

The most important lower-body ingredient of a good serve is balance. Good servers are balanced throughout a serve. You should be so well balanced that at any point throughout the service motion, right up until the point of contact, you should be able to stop and freeze and hold that position. If you can't, you're out of balance.

My suggestion is first to learn to serve with no foot movement at all. Later you can move the feet. But when your serve starts to go, minimize your foot movement to regain your service rhythm.

There is a theory that you should be off balance as you serve. All your weight should be going into the court. That might work if you only played indoors or you always had a perfect toss. But you'll still often hear a coach erroneously tell his student, "The toss is the most important part of the serve." It is if you're an off-balance server because, if the toss is a millimeter off target, the server cannot recover and hit the ball.

WAIT WITH YOUR WEIGHT ON THE BACK FOOT

Most players start their serve with the weight on their lead foot. When they begin to toss they lean backward and all their weight and momentum goes with them. It then becomes very tough for them to get their weight going forward at the right time. Instead, you should *wait* with your *weight* on the back foot.

As you're getting ready to hit up into the ball on the serve, you can either keep your feet spread a comfortable distance apart or, as Martina Navratilova does, slide the back foot up close to the front foot. Both are correct. Some players who slide the back foot forward, however, tend to have more difficulty serving on windy days or if their timing is off.

Ideally the lead foot should be at a forty-five-degree angle to the baseline. Some players prefer to start with their lead foot parallel to the baseline and then turn. This is all right, although it sometimes leads to an overrotation of the hips and shoulders as the body tries to compensate for the feet. One position you should avoid is having the feet pointing directly perpendicular to the baseline; it's an unstable position for the lead leg.

ANCHOR THE LEAD FOOT

Many pro players have a problem with their lead foot when serving. The lead foot should be the *anchor* of your serve. When everything is off, the lead foot is the steadying influence, the place where your balance begins.

If you raise the front toe on the serve, the timing of the toss becomes critical. If it's off at all, your serve will be off too. Any wind or nervousness, any loss of rhythm, and your serve can go. Even good servers like Slobodan Zivojinovic, Kevin Curren, and Boris Becker have inconsistent serves because they lift their lead toe.

KEEP A FORTY-FIVE-DEGREE ANGLE ON THE FRONT FOOT

Premature upper body turn is often the result of incorrect positioning of the front foot. If the feet come around too soon they will turn the hips, which will turn the upper part of the body prematurely in the service motion.

The ideal position is to have your front foot at approximately a forty-five-degree angle to the baseline. If you have your foot parallel to the line, you neutralize the collateral ligaments meant to support the knee. If your front foot's at a ninety-degree angle to the baseline, your hips are too open, your body is facing the court, and all you can do is push the ball over the net.

One of the keys on your
service motion is to make
sure that your lead foot
stays at a forty-five-degree
angle throughout the en-
tire serve, right up until
the point where you have
stepped into the court with
your back foot.

Balance on the serve is essential, not only throughout the serve, but also immediately afterward. In this sequence the player is falling off to the left. Not only does this lead to an erratic serve, it also forces the server to use recovery steps to get ready for the opponent's return.

Lifting the toe of your lead foot on your serve will usually result in an inconsistent serve. The lead toe is your anchor throughout the complicated serving movements and should remain in contact with the ground all through the serve. When you lift the lead toe the body can also easily fall out of balance.

An excellent way to practice hitting up on your serve is to stand six to eight feet behind a fence and try to hit the serve into the near service box. If it does not clear the fence it means you do not have the idea of hitting up on your serve.

EXPLODE UP INTO THE BALL

The common denominator of good servers is that they have a slow start, then accelerate as they begin to hit the ball. They toss the ball slowly and then explode. It's a gradual buildup. They don't have quick, jerky motions on either the toss or the racquet motion.

The important point, though, is to explode up into the ball, which creates a heavy ball. And the key to exploding into the ball is to bend your knees *as you prepare to hit up*, not as you toss. Many players bend their knees as they toss. All this does is create an inconsistent toss. The idea is to toss, then bend your knees and explode upward, launching yourself into the serve. Take a look at Becker's knee bend on his serve. It's the primary reason he has one of the most powerful serves on the tour.

SET UP QUICKLY FOR THE OVERHEAD

The elbow of the racquet arm should be up when preparing to hit an overhead. The racquet head can be anywhere, but if your racquet elbow is pointing to the sky, you will always be ready to swing.

Since the ball is rapidly gaining speed as it falls, it is difficult to judge when the ball is at the proper height to swing. So, the left hand should point at the ball as a guide to help your depth perception.

Stand sideways to the ball. Trying to hit an overhead while facing the net is as difficult to do as facing the net while serving. Without the proper shoulder turn you lose most of your potential for power. Remember, it's called the overhead smash, not the overhead poop. Hit the ball with the intention of putting it away.

Never take a full windup for an overhead. Get the racquet in the back scratcher position quickly. This shortening of the backswing for an overhead adds consistency without sacrificing a lot of power.

REACH UP, SNAP DOWN

Once you are properly prepared, remind yourself to reach up and snap down. Most overhead errors arise because the player swings after the ball has dropped too low (because the player misjudges the rapidly accelerating ball), which causes the ball to land in the net. Or hitting too long, because he did not snap his wrist downward while contacting the ball, which causes the ball to be hit long. A stiff, locked wrist inevitably causes a long hit and is usually caused by a lack of confidence.

A FEW MORE TIPS ABOUT THE OVERHEAD

There are only two types of overhead smashes—the flat and the slice. If you want power use the flat. If you want accuracy and control use the slice, but keep in mind that the slice is a difficult shot to hit consistently.

Remember, with the overhead smash you have a much larger area to hit into than you do with the serve. Use the whole court.

For good overheads I like to stress that players hit deep to their opponent's backhand. Placement is often more important than power on the overhead.

When practicing the overhead smash one thing that players do not do well is return to the ideal volley position after hitting the overhead. Therefore, when drilling, practice alternating a

To hit the overhead, first practice pointing at the ball with your left hand. Now try catching it with your left hand. Then just tap the ball with a straight right arm. Do not swing. Isolate the wrist as in the serve and hit the ball by snapping the wrist. Again, do not swing. Finally, take a full swing at the ball and smash it away! At point of contact, the right arm should be perfectly straight and the wrist loose and accelerating through the ball to generate power.

volley with an overhead. This forces you to develop the correct movement up and back. Many people become very lazy when practicing the overhead.

FOUR TIMES YOU LET THE BALL BOUNCE ON AN OVERHEAD

There are four basic times when you should consider letting the ball bounce before you hit an overhead:

1. When the ball is lobbed very high
2. When the ball is lobbed very deep
3. When it's very windy
4. When the sun is in your eyes

The overhead is the one stroke with which there isn't much room for adjustment once you start to swing. So, when the ball has the potential to go off course (in a stiff wind) or is very difficult to judge (when the ball is lobbed very high or deep or the sun is in your eyes), let it bounce, step up, and smash it away.

When you are ready to smash the overhead, it is important that you learn to jump as you hit it. This allows you to cover more court and helps you to regain control of your body quickly after backpedaling.

CHAPTER 11

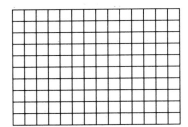

MANAGING THE LOB AND THE DROPSHOT

LOBBING IS SMART

Players who lob are intelligent players. The lob is not just a desperation shot when all else fails or a shot only girls try. The lob is both a set-up shot and an offensive weapon. For example, it is the only shot you should hit when a player crowds the net, because he's cut off most of your angles and avenues for a passing shot, and he's in too close to successfully cover even a mediocre lob. Also, it's often a good idea to lob frequently in the beginning of the match just to see if your opponent can even hit an overhead and also to show him you know how to lob. If you never lob, your opponent can crowd the net, and if he does this, you'll have trouble hitting your passing shot. The player who never lobs, therefore, is one of the easiest players to beat.

Remember, club hackers apologize for using the lob. Champions use it to win matches.

CHECKPOINTS FOR THE LOB

THE HAND AND RACQUET FINISH ABOVE YOUR HEAD

How high you follow through depends on several variables —the wind, the height of your opponent, and whether you're hitting an offensive or defensive lob—but both your hand and your racquet should finish above your head. Outdoors, if the wind is at your back, the apex of the ball's flight (that is, the top of its arc) should be closer to you, and if you're hitting into the wind the apex should be farther back, on the other side of the net. Against a very tall opponent, make sure you aim higher, which means finishing higher. And, finally, an offensive lob should get quickly over the opponent's reach, so it's generally hit with a lower arc than a defensive lob. Offensive lobs are hit with topspin.

Remember, a lob is a ground stroke, and all the principles of good ground strokes apply, including the use of the left or non-racquet hand to open and close the racquet face for more or less height, contact area to add depth, and balance.

MANAGING THE DROPSHOT

The main thing to remember on a dropshot is that the ball should have a good arc. Many players mistakenly believe a dropshot should be hit flat (without an arc), so it gets there faster and thus gives the opponent less time to get to the ball. In the first place, the dropshot is not meant to be a winner. It may, in fact, be a winner, but it should be seen as a *set-up shot*. You should have in mind that your opponent will get to the ball just before the second bounce, which means he will be close to the net and be forced to hit the ball up. That enables you to either volley his return if you move into the net or pass more easily from the baseline. On a successful dropshot, then, the ball bounces at least twice, preferably three times, inside the service box. Therefore, all dropshots are hit with backspin, because backspin pulls the ball toward the first bounce. Former Wimbledon champ Manuel Santana had so much backspin on his dropshots that he could often make the ball hop back over to his side of the net for an outright winner. Backspin also keeps the ball low, which forces your opponent to contact the ball below the level of the net. If he contacts the ball above the net and he's at the net, he's in the double-offensive position, which means he'll probably end the point on that shot.

If you always take a short backswing your opponent will know what's coming. Remember, the entire success of a dropshot is determined by how well you've disguised it. So make sure you prepare to hit the dropshot just as if you were going to hit a regular ground stroke. In fact, they should look identical up to the point of contact.

The proper way to hit a dropshot is to first make contact behind the ball and then rotate the wrist under until the strings point to the sky. The more the wrist is rotated so that the strings turn under the ball, the greater will be the backspin. The racquet ends up at the level you contacted the ball (usually waist level) with the racquet face open. Keep the wrist firm but flexible and the arm bent. A dropshot is a delicate shot, and the feel or touch it takes to properly execute such a shot cannot be taught. It comes, first of all, through the understanding of contact area. And there will be many days (even after you understand contact area) when you won't have the proper touch because of high winds, a fast court, or because your opponent hits with so much spin or pace that your touch vanishes.

FIVE TIMES YOU SELDOM HIT A DROPSHOT

Basically, there are five times when you seldom hit a dropshot:

1. Against a hard-hit ball
2. When the wind is at your back
3. On a fast surface
4. Against a high-bouncing ball
5. When you're behind the baseline

When the ball is hit hard or when you're playing on a fast surface, it is much more difficult to feel the ball and therefore it's more difficult to make a dropshot. Also, on a fast surface or when the wind is at your back, the ball tends to skid toward your opponent, making the all-important second bounce land too deep. When the ball is bouncing high above your shoulder or when you're behind the baseline, your shot must travel a long distance in the air, thus giving your opponent plenty of time to take the ball above the white band and put it away.

Also, if you know the five basic times when a player should seldom try a dropshot, you can prevent your opponent from wearing you out with them. Hit deep, which will give you plenty of time to get to his dropshots, or add more pace, which will hinder your opponent's feel for the ball.

THE COUNTER DROPSHOT

The answer when your opponent hits a good dropshot is to counter dropshot or hit a shot deep down the line. To do this successfully you must be able to hit the dropshot and the deep down-the-line shot with the same preparation. In other words, you must be able to disguise both shots. Your racquet preparation should be the same for both shots, but for the deep shot you simply lengthen the contact area, and for a dropshot you turn under the ball.

CHECKPOINTS FOR THE DROPSHOT

The checkpoints for the dropshot are relatively simple:

1. Finish with the strings pointing up to the sky and the racquet face parallel to the ground.
2. Make the ball bounce at least twice inside the service box, preferably three or four times.

Also, if you want to develop a great dropshot, play hours and hours of minitennis.

CHAPTER 12

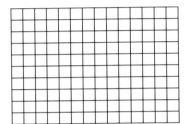

DEVELOPING YOUR GAME

FUNDAMENTALS—THE FIRST FLOOR

We've all seen the player who seems to have it all, who can bang the ball off both sides and has a potent serve and pretty good touch. But he can't play. He can't seem to put it all together, while other players make the most of limited technical abilities. Why is that? Well, a lot of it has to do with how you go about building your game.

The first floor of anyone's game should be fundamentals. I wrote this book for beginners right on up to the top touring pros. It's intended for every player on every level. In 1987 I was coaching a group of club players in Hawaii and at the same time I was helping out Bettina Bunge, a top-ten player. I taught those C and B club players exactly as I taught Bettina.

The only thing that should change as you get better is the quality of your play and the quality and versatility of your strokes. A fundamental is a fundamental is a fundamental. If it is a true fundamental it will apply from the first time you step on the court to the day you hold up the champion's trophy at Wimbledon. The quality of your play will get better and better, but the fundamentals should never change.

The sad truth is that many of the pro players on the tour today are not well-grounded in the fundamentals of the game. Oh, they can kill that ball. That's for certain. But they don't have a basic understanding of the strokes or the game itself. And it really starts to tell when their game begins to fall apart. When their forehand crumbles, for instance, they don't know what to do. A player will look at his racquet with a mystified look on his face. He hasn't got a clue why he just hit the back fence three times in a row. It's the understanding of the game and the grasp of its fundamentals that is the difference between being number ten in the world and number one hundred.

If you're going to build a ten-story building the most important floor is the first floor. That's the foundation of the whole building. Oh, that top story with the revolving restaurant might be the crowning glory, but without a solid foundation, tragedy is just around the corner. The same thing applies to your game. The foundation has to be sound if it is to support a big game.

I blame the poor foundations of most players' games today on the teaching pros. Far too many pros teach for today, not the future. They teach a lesson that gives the student a lot of instant success, but they don't teach any permanent foundation on which to build his game. If a pro puts his student right up on top of the net with a forehand grip and feeds him balls, it won't take long before he really starts to blast those balls away for great-looking volley winners. The student walks away from that lesson with a big smile, and the pro's got a happy customer and an easy buck in his pocket. But all the pro has really done is taught the student how to hit setups. The reality is if you stand on top of the net with a forehand grip, you are vulnerable to the simplest lob because you're too close to the net and you're vulnerable to a low ball because a forehand grip forces you to volley with a flat racquet face or an awkward wrist position, which translates into a lot of balls hit into the net.

The fundamentals have been ignored in favor of instant gratification at the expense of the student's future. And that's sad. The good teaching pro values the opportunity to teach and cares about the long-term success of his students.

There are a lot of other quick-fix gimmicks that teaching pros use to keep the student happy, for a while at least. But a fundamental can be built on forever. You don't have to go backward. To hit a good volley, for example, you've got to hit it one-handed. If you've developed a two-handed backhand volley because it was easier in the beginning, all you've done is develop a weakness you may never overcome. And, believe me, the better opponents you play, the more they will spot and exploit that weakness.

Other coaches tell you to change grips when going from the backhand to forehand volley and when you get stronger you can go to a one-grip approach. It sounds reasonable, except that bad habits are very difficult to break once they're ingrained. And that can mean death to a player's future. Why build a game on a fundamentally unsound structure that you'll simply have to tear down when you want to improve past the intermediate stage? Thinking you can change your game later is an illusion.

INDIVIDUALITY—BUILDING ON YOUR STRENGTHS

People always ask me, "What is an advanced game?" My answer is that there is no such thing. There are only advanced players. I'm not playing a word game. Some players walk out on the court their very first day and have a monster serve. That's considered an advanced shot for most players, but they are not advanced players.

See, everybody has their own strengths. Some people are fast. Some are smart. Some are great game players. Those are strengths, and if strong enough, they could be incorporated directly into the game of a top-hundred player. And it would make that world-class pro a better player.

But I don't believe in an advanced game per se. Everybody is an individual. I know thousands of players who have been able to volley better than Björn Borg, but they never won five Wimbledon titles. Of course, they didn't have Borg's speed, stamina, ferocious will to win, and power ground strokes. If you just judged Borg on his volley alone, he was a mediocre player. There are lots of club players who could outvolley Borg.

How about Jimmy Connors's serve? Many club players have better serves than Connors. But have there been many better all-round players than Jimbo in the entire history of the game? Or take Stefan Edberg's forehand. It's a very limited shot under pressure. Most college players today who have built their game around the semi-Western forehand could push Edberg off the court if all he could do was hit a forehand.

These three players, all Wimbledon champs, are some of the best to ever play. And yet certain parts of their games would not be considered advanced. What if Borg's coach had told him you can't go anywhere unless you can volley, then threw him off the Swedish Junior Team? Sweden would have been deprived of eleven grand-slam titles and the Borg legacy of the countless Swedish champions who followed him: Wilander, Edberg, Nystrom, Jarryd, and so on.

So, what's the point? Well, it's simple really. There is no such thing as an advanced game—only advanced players. Every player has strengths that he builds his game around. Parts of his game will be extraordinary, others mediocre to downright bad. There is no signature of an advanced game. Each player creates his own game.

One of the primary requirements of a good coach is that they must use their eyes and ears before they use their mouth when instructing. They must first observe the student to see what he's got naturally—what his potential is, what he likes to do, and what his natural strengths are. You don't build a running game for a slow-footed player with a big serve. The most important thing is to observe the student. If you don't you're not teaching a person, you're teaching a system that pays no attention to the individual and his game, his strengths and weaknesses.

One particular woman who took lessons from me was a good example of how to teach an individual as an individual. The first day on court I asked her what sports she had played before tennis?

"None," she said.

Usually, a beginning tennis player has participated in at least one other sport before they take up tennis. But not in her case. So I asked her what other pastimes she enjoyed.

"Well," she said, "I used to be a musician. I played the violin."

So I taught her to hit spin by the sound of the ball. That's right. I had her close her eyes and showed her what topspin sounds like and then what backspin sounds like. Then I had her attempt to simulate it, and she was hitting with spin within five minutes.

Here was a lady who was slow, nonathletic, with no real interest in doing anything more than playing the odd social doubles game and hitting around with her husband and kids someday. That's it. That was her goal.

If I taught a system instead of the individual, I would have had her out there learning some complicated backhand shot that she would never, *never* have used.

Individuality is a foundation of a player's game. That's why I don't teach a system but individuals.

Freedom goes hand in hand with individuality. Players should have the freedom to explore their abilities, whereas most teaching concepts inhibit you from exploration. When I develop tennis players I develop them without putting any ceilings on their games. A primary foundation of my students' game, then, is their innate capabilities. For a woman who is five foot one, it may be the bounce in her step that is her strength. She may not be fast, but she can move like a tennis player.

The idea is to build on your strengths, to build your arsenal of weapons according to *your* game. That's why I can't sit here and tell you step by step how to construct your game—everyone's game is different.

Are you fast? Then great court coverage should be an important part of your game. Do you have a powerful throwing arm? Then you can build your game around a powerful serve. You might think about building a big serve-and-volley game. But then, if you're slow and overweight, that's probably not your best game plan even though you've got a big serve.

If you can't hit a serve over fifty miles per hour, I don't

recommend building your game around an attacking serve-and-volley game. Some people, however, love the net, feel comfortable there, and have the athletic ability to cover any shot hit at them. They should probably develop a strong net game. Hitting a penetrating approach shot and getting in behind it should be their plan of attack.

This book is meant to build the player from the inside out. How do you feel about yourself and your game? What are *your* strengths physically and mentally? What is your temperament? This book demands a lot of its readers. I am asking you to really think about yourself and your game. Otherwise, half of the benefits this book offers will be lost to you.

IDENTIFYING YOUR STRENGTHS

Many times I'll ask a player what his strengths are and he doesn't really know. There is often a lot of difference between what a player thinks are his strengths and what they really are.

One of the first things you should notice is whether your game is sound defensively. Do you have a game you can count on under pressure? A strength is not a strength if it's going to fall apart under pressure. Edberg's forehand is actually pretty consistent when there's no pressure on him. He'll breeze through a 6–2, 6–1 match with absolutely no problem. Then he'll get to the quarters or semis of the tournament and the better players will begin to exploit his forehand because they know how to do it.

If you can hit a big backhand in warm-up but as soon as the opponent comes to the net in a match you can't get the ball over the net, it's not a strength. The number-one characteristic of a strength is that it is reliable under pressure.

FLEXIBILITY

Everybody has strengths. Of course, if you play Ivan Lendl he can make even your most reliable strength, your favorite shot, look like a weakness. And that's an important point. If you play someone who has a great return of serve, who forces you on every shot, then suddenly that big strength, your booming serve, won't help you much. Now you've got to adjust your thinking. The dumb player just keeps blasting away. He just hits that serve harder and harder no matter what happens. But if you're smart you'll rethink your game plan.

It's also important to assess your own game each day. Some days that big forehand that you just love to hit won't go in. It happens all the time, even to the very best players. You never know from day to day what tennis game you'll show up with.

That's why you've got to assess your game when you get on

the court each day. How do you feel? Could you run all day? Or maybe you just got done with a grueling day at work and, frankly, you're exhausted. All you really feel like is a game of hit-and-giggle doubles, but the game you've got scheduled is with the club champ.

One common denominator of good tennis players is that they're open-minded, they're flexible. They can easily adjust to the inevitable ups and downs on and off the court. You've got to play to your optimum every day—and your optimum changes from day to day. So that means you've got to figure out what you've got that day. What's going to work that day and what isn't. Have you got the one hundred–plus mile per hour serve, or is it just so-so today? Can you crack the forehand, or will you just have to be satisfied with spinning it in deep? You've got to know what you've got that day and work with it as best you can.

Now some days nothing can stop you. You're in the zone, and everything you touch turns into a winner. I've had those days. We all have. They're like a gift from God. A one day vacation to tennis paradise. When you're having a great day—enjoy it. Go for the lines, try the impossible shot, defy all the percentages, because on a day like that percentages mean nothing. Have a ball. But be prepared to come back down to earth the next day.

That's where many players make a mistake. They have a perfect, can't-do-anything-wrong kind of day and they think they've finally arrived. It's all come together. They blast every shot and everything goes in. They're convinced they've hit a new plateau of playing. Then they go out the next day and they can't understand why those shots aren't going in. But they just keep trying them. It might take them a month to get over that one great day.

One of the foundations of good tennis, then, is flexibility. If you're flexible you can raise your worst day so it's not so bad. You can adjust. Your worst day will never be that bad if you can say, "Oh, I don't have my forehand today—fine. What do I have today? My serve and my topspin backhand are working. I'll use those."

CREATIVITY

I was teaching Ahmad Rashad, the NFL announcer and former all-pro receiver for the Minnesota Vikings at The Woodlands in Texas a few years back. He looked very uncomfortable when hitting his forehand, which surprised me because Ahmad is a great athlete. So I stopped him and asked, "Why are you turning sideways on every shot?"

"That's what I was told. You have to turn sideways on every ground stroke."

"Can you give me any reasons why that would be so?"

"Not really," he said. "I thought that was just the way you had to do it."

"OK," I said, "then forget it."

I then had him stand still and hit balls from a completely open stance. "That feel OK, Ahmad?"

"Yeah, this feels great!"

So I had him hit a bunch of different shots, moving side to side, scrambling all around, and about three or four minutes into the drill he threw his racquet into the air and yelled, "You just let me out of prison, Peter."

And he was smiling from ear to ear.

An essential ingredient in any good player's game should be creativity, and in order to be creative you have to have the freedom to express yourself as an athlete and a tennis player. A good coach allows you to develop your own individual style. He doesn't force-feed you a lot of so-called classic form while ignoring your own capabilities and personality. If a player is a fiery type, why try to make him a nonaggressive, conservative player?

The biggest stumbling block to a creative player is often the coach. Any kind of strange shot is automatically discouraged. But when a beginning player first steps on the court, he is probably at his most creative. He may use his wrist a lot. Or open and closed stances—all the things that the very best of the world-class players use as a natural part of their game. Instead of discouraging those kinds of shots, the pro should help the player refine them and show him how they can be used. I tell my students they can do anything they want on the tennis court as long as it works and it is medically sound.

One thing, though. Don't confuse creativity with individuality, although they are closely related. Individuality is more related to the way you hit the ball—whether you're a predominantly open-stance player, whether you like to jump when you hit the ball—in short, your style.

Starting with your individual style built on a solid foundation of fundamentals, you can then experiment, see what the possibilities are. That is creativity. John McEnroe does not have classic form. He does it all his own way. He is one of the freest and most creative players to ever play the game. But fundamentally John is completely sound. So he's got it all—fundamentals, individuality, and creativity.

Now creativity can be taught. Peter Burwash International

is fortunate enough to run the national junior tennis programs in several countries, including China, Indonesia, and India. During the workouts for these teams the players do drills in which they are restricted in some way. For example, they might not be able to hit a forehand. They can hit any other shot they want, but not a forehand.

Try it with a practice partner. It forces a new understanding of the possibilities on the court. Your opponent is constantly trying to think of ways to force you out of position. So it teaches body control and creative court positioning.

The funny thing about this drill is that this is the way most beginners play anyway. They run around their backhands all the time, which puts them way out of position on almost every shot. These drills increase your creativity. You really have to get inventive and think on the court. You are forced to read your opponent and anticipate.

DEVELOPING FEEL

The essence of creativity is feel. Most players think feel is all those offensive touch, or finesse, shots, difficult to execute and only for the best players. But actually feel develops from a sound defensive foundation. You see, most touch shots are hit with backspin—the basis of the defensive game. You don't really feel topspin because that's your power spin. It may look like a good shot, but it's on your strings for so short a time you can't really say you feel it.

The key to feel, then, is to learn backspin, because most of the touch shots are backspin—dropshots, lobs, dinks. There are no topspin dropshots, for instance. You can hit a topspin lob but that is not a touch shot. It's a powerful offensive weapon.

Many players play for a long time and never develop any feel. But from their very first day on the court I teach my students feel. It shouldn't take a player five years before he understands touch. He should begin to feel the ball right away. The sooner you know what the ball feels like when it hits the strings, the better player you will become. The most important thing in learning the serve, for example, is not to hit it hard, but to get the feel of a topspin serve, the feel of the ball on the strings as you hit it.

Even though he's dropped in the rankings, McEnroe is still the king of touch on the tour today. He uses his hand to work the ball. What makes him a champion is what Laver and Ashe and other great champions had. When they got in trouble they had the ability to turn a defensive position into an offensive one with one shot. And they did it with their hands. Inherently, when in trouble you're in a position you don't want to be in. You're in an unnatural position hitting an unnatural shot, and there's only one way you can get out of it—by using your wrist. No other part of your body can move that fast.

One final thing. Creativity is developed within the context of practice. You don't all of a sudden decide to become a creative player in the middle of a tournament match. When learning to play the piano, for example, you must first learn the fundamentals of keystroking. The creativity comes after you can play that piece. You can then put feeling into the music. That feeling, that creativity, that flavor to your game, is the element that puts you a cut above the average player.

COMPETITION

The final element in developing your game is to play a lot of tennis. Nothing improves your game like competition. Even the easiest match can help build your game. The key is knowing how to compete. Each match you play, whether you win handily or are trounced, should be a learning experience. If you're thoroughly dominating a match, it's a good time to work on your game. Having trouble with your topspin serve? Hit nothing but second serves. Are your touch shots vanishing under pressure? Work on them. Don't just blast your way through the match and walk off as dumb as when you walked on the court.

The best situation, of course, is when you're in a high-pressure match. The game is on the line, and you're playing someone who pushes you to the limit without blowing you off the court.

That is why I highly recommend tournament tennis, it's where the real pressure is. If you lose, you go home. That's how you learn what your true strengths and true weaknesses are. And not just how you hit the ball, but how you react under pressure. Competition is the testing ground for your game. If your game is not fundamentally solid, tournament tennis will shake it to its foundations.

SET TWO

PLAYING YOUR OPPONENT'S COURT: THE STRATEGY FOR THE TOTAL GAME

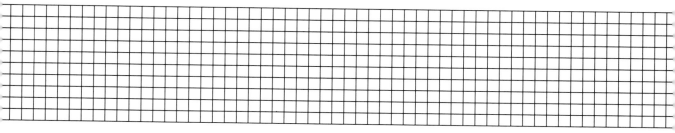

PART I
THE FOUNDATIONS OF STRATEGY

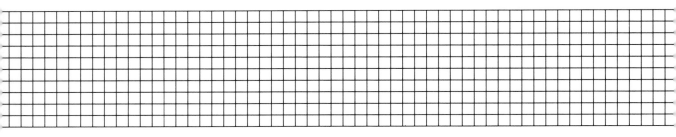

CHAPTER 13

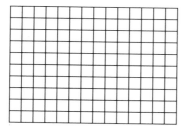

DEVELOPING TRIPLE VISION

In all my years of teaching tennis, I have never said to a student, "Watch the ball!" It is the most overworked cliché in tennis. But not only is it a cliché, it is also incorrect! Most tennis players are so worried about watching the ball that they've got tunnel vision. Their minds are zeroed in on that little space where the ideal ball is supposed to be hit.

But let's use some common sense. There are three foundations, three necessary elements to the game of tennis—a ball, a court, and an opponent. To play a good game of tennis you must learn to focus on all three of these elements and develop what I call triple vision.

A good driver is continually looking in the side- and rearview mirrors and yet continues to drive straight ahead because he has in his head a visual image of what's in front of him. In other words, he's using triple vision. The same idea applies in tennis. You should be looking at the court and your opponent at all times. You don't have to constantly look at the ball to know where it is. Most of the time a watch-the-ball addict has no idea where his opponent is or where the potential openings on the court are. His head is down, all his attention on the ball, and suddenly his opponent sneaks to the net. The first time he suspects anything's wrong is when he sees the ball hit the other guy's racquet for a winner.

If you study pictures of McEnroe he is almost never watching the ball. His vision is always six to eight feet out in front of him. That's why John has a great sense of what and where everything is on the court.

Interestingly, the California Highway Patrol ran an experiment on drunk drivers to test their vision. It was found that an inebriated driver looks at only one thing. That is, his gaze is fixated on one object in front of him. Whereas the eyes of a driver in charge of all his faculties are dancing all over the place. He is aware of many, many things in front of and in back of him. If you're only looking at the ball when you're on the court, you're playing as if you're stone drunk.

Multiple vision is stressed in all sports. In football you see the defense constantly juggling, anticipating, trying to read their opponents by the position of their feet and shoulders or a dozen other things. Likewise in basketball, a man on defense is always aware of his man, the ball, and his teammates, and yet at all times he keeps his back to the goal, so he's aware of his court position. In fact, multiple vision is taught in most sports, but in tennis the fallacy persists that if you zero in on the ball your problems are over.

The most important thing to understand in order to progress in tennis is triple vision. Triple vision is more difficult to learn than only watching the ball, but if you want a future in tennis, you must develop an awareness of all three dimensions of the game. In other words, if you want to get better, if you've been stuck on a plateau for a year, two years, or ten years, the quickest way off that plateau is through the understanding of triple vision. Because if you understand the three foundations of the game, every bit of tennis knowledge and strategy and technique follows from there.

I think the best way to begin to learn triple vision is in a group. I have my students act as the teaching pro and toss balls to the other students. I ask them to observe several things as the other player hits the ball—their body, their feet, their racquet preparation, the angle of their racquet face, and their stroke.

There are also a couple of useful drills that will help you develop triple vision. First, try a dual-vision drill that helps you observe two things at once. Have a friend bounce you two tennis balls simultaneously. Reach out and catch them both, one in each hand, at the same time. When you've mastered that, try catching them by crossing your hands one over the other.

Next, try a triple-vision drill. Have a friend toss you two balls at the same time. Catch one with your nonracquet hand and hit the other back to the tosser. To make it even more challenging, the tosser can move right, left, forward, or backward after tossing. You have to be aware of your opponent and each of the balls to do this drill.

A great way to start learning triple vision is to play a lot of minitennis.

CHAPTER 14

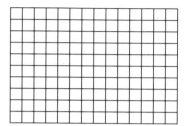 ## BALL AWARENESS—THE FIRST FOUNDATION

There are three areas of ball awareness: spin, the height of the ball, and the ball itself.

SPIN

Many people play tennis for years and never learn the first thing about spin—how to hit it or how to handle it. In fact, when I first started teaching tennis, I was told not to teach people how to hit with spin for at least two years. But there are several important reasons to hit with spin. Perhaps the most important is that only two things make the ball land in the court: gravity and spin. Beginners use gravity to vary depth in their opponent's court by hitting harder or softer; more advanced players use spin. The pros can hit the ball very hard and make it stay in because they use spin. But contrary to what most club players believe, it is not just for power. It should be used principally to gain control over the ball.

You can vary both the depth and the height of the ball through spin. But more important, you should use more spin in emergencies, particularly backspin, because the ball travels more slowly and gives you more time to recover. Also, backspin is your control spin (topspin is your power spin), and you must try for maximum control in emergencies.

How to handle a spinning ball is another matter. Beginners watch the ball bounce and then react, and that's what causes those quick, jerky motions typical of a beginning player. Professionals are rarely fooled, however, because they learn to recognize the different spins and how each will react. The fundamental rule in understanding spin is that backspin bounces lower and topspin bounces higher. Also, backspin will tend to float and topspin will dip quickly back down toward the court.

DRILLS TO UNDERSTAND SPIN

1. If you're a beginner, have a player who understands and uses spin hit a lot of different spins to you so you can observe what happens. Just stand there and watch. A ball with heavy topspin bouncing at the service line will land past the baseline; one with heavy backspin bouncing at the service line will land inside the baseline; sidespin will act like backspin, but tends to curve the ball right or left.

The conclusion of this drill is to watch your opponent's racquet face to see what it does on each type of shot. At first it will take you a full second or two to recognize the type of spin by what the racquet does, but eventually your recognition will be instantaneous.

2. Now have your friend hit various spins at you and try to catch each ball at waist level. A topspin lob will force you to sprint to the fence to catch it, a dropshot will have you racing to the net. But because you don't have to worry about how or where you're going to hit the ball, you can concentrate fully on reading the different spins.

THE HEIGHT OF THE BALL

Generally, on a medium-paced ball, the height at which the ball clears the net relates to how deep it lands in the court. Most people, however, have no idea what's going to happen when the ball goes high or low over the net. Generally, a ball that clears the net by a lot will land deep and a ball that barely clears the net will land short. Obviously, this varies according to the speed and trajectory.

A good player can determine what the height of the ball will be as soon as his opponent hits it, or at the very latest as it crosses the net. That's why on a let-cord shot (a ball that skips off the top of the net during a rally) a pro will often get to the ball quite easily, whereas a club player watches it fall over for a winner and mumbles to himself how lucky his opponent is. The reason the pro gets to the ball has nothing to do with luck, and it is not necessarily that he's that much faster than the average club player. It's just that he's anticipating better.

Here's a drill that will improve your ball awareness almost immediately. Divide your side of the court up into three areas by placing racquet covers at the sidelines to mark off the following:

1. Up close to the net (about five or six feet back)
2. In the middle
3. Very deep

As soon as the ball leaves the opponent's racquet, call out "1," "2," or "3" according to the area in which you think the ball will land. In the beginning you'll often be wrong, but after ten or fifteen minutes you'll begin to pinpoint where the ball will land. Imagine what this will do for your game.

THE BALL ITSELF

A tennis ball will react differently according to the type of ball, the type of surface, and the elements, including wind and altitude. There are dozens of different brands of balls—Wilson, Penn, Slazenger, Dunlop, and Nassau, to name a few—and they all play a little differently. Some bounce high, some tend to float, some are fast, and some are slow. There are also many specific types of balls: hard-core, heavy-duty nap, and nonpressurized balls usually tend to play slower and heavier, while soft-core, regular-nap, and pressurized balls usually have added pace and a tendency to float.

Hit a few of the match balls in warm-up and try to adjust your game accordingly. For example, a very heavy, nonpressurized ball will tend to neutralize power serves and prolong rallies. A serve-and-volley game, therefore, becomes less effective. Most professionals know the type of ball being used in a tournament before they even arrive for their first match. That's how important the type of ball is to a match. If there's time, pros practice in advance on the *surface* to be used for an upcoming tournament, along with using the balls.

The court surface is a significant factor in the way the ball will react. A clay court will "grab" the ball and make it bounce more slowly than a grass or hard court. This means on clay you can track down a lot more balls that would be outright winners on other surfaces. On grass the ball often takes erratic bounces. You never really know what it will do, except that most shots stay extremely low, sometimes never coming up at all. Conversely, hard courts usually yield a steady, "true" bounce. The important thing is to get out before a match and experience the court surface and note how the ball reacts to the court.

Finally, you should be aware of what altitude can do to a tennis ball. A fair percentage of the world's population lives at a significant altitude.

In the rarefied air at high altitudes, the ball takes off. A player who goes from the mountains to sea level to play will have less trouble keeping the ball in than usual, as long as he gets the ball over the net. But if you go from sea level to the mountains (any altitude over three thousand feet), which is more common since most of us live near sea level, then you'll have trouble, especially for the first hour. The best way to adjust quickly is to aim all your shots at the service line—they'll land around the baseline. In fact, there are a few circuit players who sometimes go to train at high altitude because it builds the lung capacity and forces you to gain better control over the ball.

CHAPTER 15

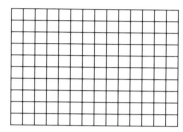

COURT AWARENESS—THE SECOND FOUNDATION

Understanding the possibilities of the court—in other words, court awareness—is an essential step in becoming a good player. Common sense will tell you that if you don't understand the court, you won't understand tennis.

Court awareness does not come naturally even to an athlete. Very few times have I seen a beginner come out and grasp court awareness immediately. A beginner sees only a bunch of lines. Gradually, however, he learns there is a forecourt and backcourt, a deuce and advantage service box. But there is much more to the court than meets the untutored eye.

THE SEVEN TARGET ZONES

There are actually seven basic target zones on the court: the two deep corners, the two dropshot or drop-volley corners (those corners closest to the net), and the three "T's"—the two side T's, where the service line meets the two sidelines, and the center T, where the center line meets the service line.

After you learn these seven target zones, you must learn to hit the ball to those spots, and the best way to develop that ability is through drills.

An excellent drill to develop your court awareness is to throw the ball to the target zones in your practice partner's court. Your partner must catch the ball on one bounce or in the air. He then throws the next "shot" and the points are played out in this manner. This drill develops your awareness of the possibilities on the court. It's also great for conditioning.

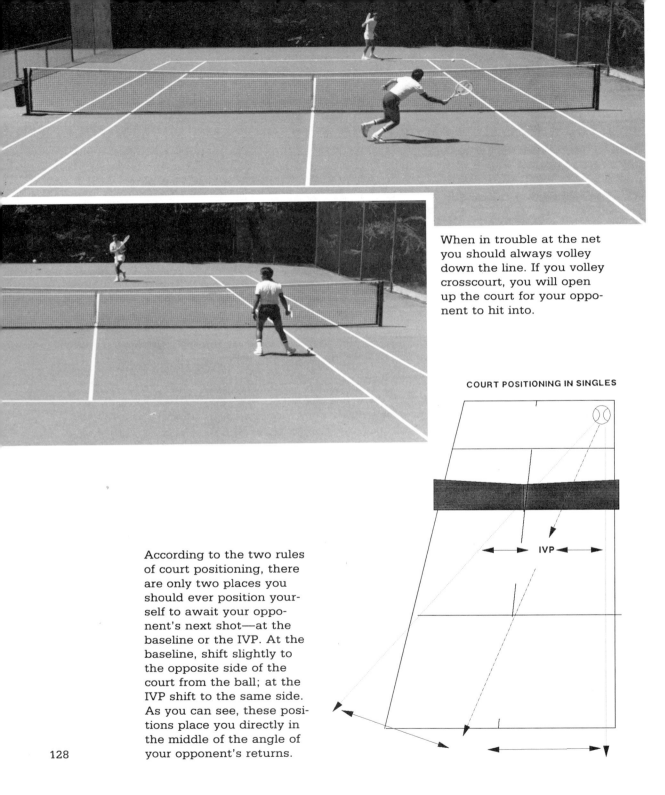

When in trouble at the net you should always volley down the line. If you volley crosscourt, you will open up the court for your opponent to hit into.

COURT POSITIONING IN SINGLES

IVP

According to the two rules of court positioning, there are only two places you should ever position yourself to await your opponent's next shot—at the baseline or the IVP. At the baseline, shift slightly to the opposite side of the court from the ball; at the IVP shift to the same side. As you can see, these positions place you directly in the middle of the angle of your opponent's returns.

Then have one player play with a racquet and one without, and finally have both players use racquets.

Next, try calling out the number of the target zone you're hitting to *before* you hit the ball. For advanced players, have a coach or friend call out the number of the target zone just before you hit so you have to "hold" your shot until the last second. This is also great for disguise as well as court awareness.

THE TWO RULES OF COURT POSITIONING

Court awareness is understanding things such as angles and target zones. But it is also understanding that the court position of both you and your opponent determines those angles and those possible target zones. The singles court is only twenty-seven feet wide, so most people can get to the ball as long as they know the simple strategic approach to standing in the proper position.

Basically there are two rules covering 95 percent of all positioning problems. When the ball is in your opponent's court:

1. Get back either to the ideal volley position (IVP), halfway between the service line and the net, or to the baseline after each shot. (This law is only broken on a first volley when serving and volleying, or if you're forced back on an overhead and can't regain the IVP. First volleys are usually taken around the service line, the defensive volley position, or DVP.)

2. Shift slightly to the opposite side of the court from where your opponent is about to hit the ball when you're at the baseline, and to the same side when you're at the net.

These two positioning rules place you in the center of where the greatest number of balls will likely be hit, and therefore they are the ideal positions from which to get most shots. Of course, if your opponent can only hit crosscourt, which is common with beginning and intermediate players, then by all means cheat crosscourt, where you know the ball is probably coming.

If you follow these rules you will rarely be caught out of position. And that will immediately improve your game, because most intermediate and beginning players are almost always out of position.

When you come to the net and hit your volley or your approach shot to the corner, you should stand two to three feet off the center service line on the same side to which you hit the ball. Normally, a player at the net has time to take only one crossover step, but that's usually enough. This leaves only a very small opening for the opponent to hit a down-the-line passing shot.

THE MOST FEARED OPPONENTS—
WIND AND SUN

THE WIND

Most tennis players put a high sun and a gusty wind in the same category as pestilence and famine. If it's windy on the day of the match, mysterious injuries are claimed that suddenly vanish the next day. In Hawaii, where the sun is very bright and hot, there are many players who can't play between eleven and one because the sun destroys their "perfect toss." There are thousands of available excuses to latch onto in tennis: blisters, marital problems, bad-fitting shoes, too much to eat, too little to eat, and on and on.

When I played the South African Sugar Circuit in the late 1960s, one of the stops was Port Elizabeth, and the wind was so strong there that I once tossed the ball too high and the wind threw it back over the fence into a garage behind the court. In a small town in the Middle East there were hundreds of kids outside the stadium, and their favorite game was to loft stones inside and see if they could hit one of the players. There was always heavy wagering among these delinquents. In the South

If you're in the proper volley position, your opponent has a little more area in which to pass crosscourt, but it's still not an easy shot. In order to hit that angle he must hit the ball a little softer or put a little more spin on it so it won't carry long. That means the ball will travel slower, giving you a little more time to intercept his shot.

Pacific we played on courts composed of coral, and if you fell tournament personnel had to take a wire brush and scrape the wound clean to prevent infection. (The coral would actually grow in the wound if you left it.) This preyed heavily on my mind, particularly since the footing on coral is not the best.

So there are always plenty of problems on the court, but the worst problem you can encounter in tennis is a bad attitude. Imagine the advantage a player automatically gains if he loves playing in the wind and his opponent hates it. The match is just about over, and that one mental difference will overcome nearly anything.

If you never say "I hate playing in the wind" again, you will win 75 percent of your matches on a windy day before you even hit the ball over the net, because your opponent will be concentrating so hard on his fear and loathing he will forget how to hit the ball.

The San Francisco Giants have played in windy Candlestick Park for more than twenty-five years, and for much of that time they have lost there. But in 1985 new manager Roger Craig got rid of the complainers on the club and turned around the attitude of the rest of the Giants. Now they love to play there because Craig taught them that Candlestick is their secret weapon. Since all the visiting teams hate it there, they have a distinct advantage. The Giants had one of the best home records in baseball in 1987 and went on to win their division for the first time in over a decade. And mostly because they changed their attitude about playing in the wind and cold of San Francisco.

Do not complain or make excuses out loud about how you hate to play in the wind or on slow courts or against a "dinker." These remarks do nothing but encourage your opponent to play his best.

Think of the wind and the sun as your allies. When the wind is at your back, you don't have to hit the ball so hard. When you're hitting against the wind, you can often hit the heck out of the ball and it won't go out. A side wind will allow you to hit the ball into or away from your opponent. You can play like a king in the wind!

Always check the wind. Feel it on the back of your hands, your legs, and your face. When you play into the wind it's best to hit topspin, and when you have the wind at your back, backspin is most effective. Try not to use a lot of topspin with the wind at your back, because a topspin shot should clear the net by several feet. Since wind velocity usually increases with height, a high shot can get caught up in the wind and easily carry beyond the baseline. Backspin, though it won't dip down as quickly, can be hit lower, "below" the wind.

But keep in mind that with the wind at your back you need more control, so aim for the center T. With the wind coming at you, aim for the baseline. If you purposely try to land the ball on the baseline, you'll land it three feet inside almost every time.

When lobbing, be aware that the wind above the fence and windscreens is usually much stronger than at ground level, so the ball will really take off once you get it up in the air. Compensate according to the strength of the wind that day.

Also, on ground strokes and volleys make sure your arm is bent more at the elbow on a windy day so you can adjust more easily to a ball that suddenly flies off its normal course. Also, line up closer to the ball. A bent arm means the racquet will be closer to you.

It's very tough to volley well on a windy day because hitting a ball in the air is very unpredictable under those conditions. Sudden gusts can play a lot of nasty tricks. Also, a ball in the air moves very fast, allowing you very little time to adjust to sudden changes. If you let it bounce, however, it slows down and you can follow its flight more easily.

A swirling wind is the most difficult to play in. Fortunately, 95 percent of the time when you walk out on the court, you'll have a consistent wind. When you've got to play in a swirling wind, however, most of your focus should be on the ball rather than your opponent. But you can afford to do that because your opponent is not going to be coming to the net much or gambling a whole lot. When there's a heavy wind you should play basic, conservative tennis. You hit down the center, you stay back most of the time, and you try to get the ball back as best you can. You're not throwing up many lobs or hitting drops or fancy angles. You're just trying to hang in there and play the elements.

Serving on a windy day can actually be an advantage if you know how to adjust your toss and keep it low. The strategy is simple: when you hit into the wind utilize a lot of slice away from or into your opponent. A slice serve will stay low, while a topspin serve with a higher clearance of the net will get caught up in the wind and tend to sit up. This enables your opponent to put a lot of pressure on you. Against a slice serve, however, your opponent will have to play a low-bouncing ball that takes him out wide. He'll then have to hit the ball up with the wind at his back, and he'll be prone to hitting the ball long.

Also, when you're hitting with the wind you should hit a big serve and keep the rest of your game under tight control. When hitting into the wind, the idea is to hit a controlled serve and really blast your ground strokes.

A player who learns to play with natural movement instead of structured form will be able to adjust better under unusual conditions. For example, a server with a very structured toss will have trouble in the wind, but a player who learns to serve emphasizing the wrist will be able to adjust. In other words, a player who concentrates on the contact area and reacting to emergencies instead of relying on form will be able to handle crosswinds, bad bounces, and any other problems that occur in a match.

THE SUN

The major problems presented by a bright, high sun are seeing the ball on the serve and overheads and heat exhaustion. Those pros who insist that a perfect toss is mandatory for a good serve have been out in the sun too long. Or not long enough. They'll draw a circle at your feet and tell you to make the ball land in the circle. But what if the sun is at the exact spot where the toss must go to land in the circle? You may have the perfect toss, but it'll only be effective on perfect days—which means you'll only be able to hit a serve about ten days out of every year unless you play indoors or at night.

When serving in the sun you've got to learn to alter your toss, and that's largely a mental thing. Sure a consistent toss is an asset, but as I've said before, the key to the serve is the wrist. As far as the overhead is concerned, the best thing to do if you're blinded by the sun while hitting an overhead is to let it bounce. Shielding the eyes with the left hand also helps—or wear a sun visor.

Heat exhaustion is a real peril, and the best remedy is preparation. Be sure to bring a hat, a spare shirt, a lot of sweatbands, towels, and water. Also, be aware of your opponent. How is he holding up? There is a phenomenon known as "early-match dizziness"—the shakes—and you can beat a far superior player if you jump on him early while he's trying to adjust to a very hot day.

Also, beware of cold weather. On a hot day you can warm up and take a break before your match, but on a cold day your practice and the match should, ideally, be back to back. Taking a break on a cold day is an easy way to court injuries and chills. Also, don't play the first couple of games in your warm-ups before you take them off. As you shed clothes for greater mobility, your sweat and the sudden cold will chill your body—a great method for getting muscle pulls.

CLAY

The important thing about playing on clay is to realize from the moment you walk on the court that you're going to be there for a while. There's a joke in Europe, where they play mostly on slow red clay, that you should take your lunch to the court. Or your dinner. Or your lunch and dinner. And it's hard for a fast-living American who's used to getting the whole match over in an hour to accept the fact that just the first set may take that long.

The mental attitude for each point is similar. You figure, I'm going to serve and stay out here and hit balls back. And I'm not going to make any errors. You immediately establish the attitude that you will eliminate all mistakes. You'll do anything to get the ball over the net.

I saw a match between Bill Alvarez and Eduardo Zuleta the first year I played in Europe, and one point lasted twenty-seven minutes! Figuring 1 shot for every three seconds on clay, that point consisted of about 540 shots. You seldom hit that many shots in a whole match on a hard court.

The next stage in learning to play tennis on clay is to do something with the ball, which means using the seven target zones. The side T's are used (on clay and hard courts) for put-away volleys and as set-up areas on ground strokes to maneuver the opponent outside the doubles alley. A side-T shot leaves the court wide open, and though you may not be able to hit a winner, your opponent will probably have to run a long way to get to the next shot. If your opponent counters your shots with his own placements, then it becomes like a boxing match with both players counterpunching. That's when tennis on clay becomes very exciting.

Roy Emerson, a great clay-court player, was perhaps the fittest tennis player I've ever known. I watched him run ten miles one day—five miles forward and five backward! Running became a major part of his game. He was one of the few Australians (or anyone else for that matter) who could win on any surface. He didn't have classic strokes, but he was fit and had great court awareness.

The thing that made Emerson really great was that he was one of the few who could serve and volley on clay. There's a special technique to the serve and volley on clay. First of all, you don't serve hard. The trick is to time the speed of your serve according to your foot speed—the speed with which you can get just inside the service line and get set. (On the other hand, you can't serve too softly, either, or the opponent will pass you on the return.) If you're especially fit you can get a step or two inside the service line, which is what you have to do to serve and volley successfully on clay. And you must get balanced. You can't rush the net and try to stop abruptly or you'll end up on your face, because the footing is so uncertain on clay.

HARD COURTS

The basic strategy on a hard court is related to the speed of the surface. And on a hard court the speed runs the gamut from as fast as ice to as slow as clay; the slower the hard court is, the more you follow clay-court strategy. If the court is very fast there are few tactics or strategies involved. There's not much real stroke production, and much of the play is simply blocking the ball back. There's no such thing as finessing a guy on a very fast hard court. You seldom use a dropshot, and patience is not as important because a point usually lasts only two or three shots. The chances of exploiting an opponent's weakness, therefore, are less on a hard court. It's also a lot more difficult to hit passing shots because the ball gets to you so much faster.

GRASS COURTS

Grass is an unpredictable surface, so your emphasis is on getting to the net, volleying, taking the ball in the air, and not letting the ball bounce. That's why the Aussies, many of whom were brought up playing on grass, are geared to capturing the net. On grass, simply accept the fact that you're going to get a lot of bad bounces and you'll love it.

Sadly, grass courts and therefore grass-court tournaments are a dying phenomenon. If you ever get a chance to play on a grass court, jump at it.

PLAYING INDOORS

Playing indoors eliminates what most players consider their two main enemies—wind and sun—and it's often easier to see the ball against the consistent indoor backgrounds. The conditions on a good indoor court can be ideal, and ideal conditions enhance concentration.

There are some problems in paradise, however. The ceiling sometimes causes problems with the lob. Since most indoor courts are built with the top of the V-shaped roof over the net, you must learn to lob by having the path of the racquet follow the roofline. Practice it a few times and the low ceiling won't be a problem.

Another problem with indoor play is the injuries brought on by improper warm-up. Indoor time is expensive, so everyone wants to get right to it. But that extra five minutes of play isn't worth the money you end up paying to the doctor if you get hurt. Be sure to warm up properly.

Perhaps the biggest drawback to playing under ideal conditions indoors, however, is the shock to your game when you play outdoors and have to face the elements again.

PART II
OPPONENT AWARENESS:
THE THIRD FOUNDATION

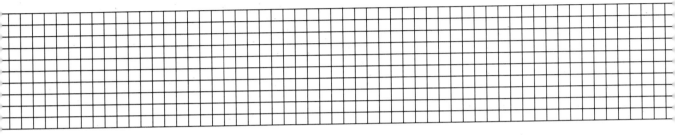

CHAPTER 16

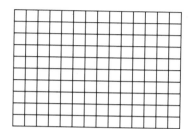

PRIVATE-EYEING YOUR OPPONENT

SHERLOCK HOLMES WOULD HAVE MADE A GREAT TENNIS PLAYER

Hitting the ball is only 30 to 40 percent of the game. If you want to get to the next level of your game, you have to be a good investigator. Think of your opponent's game as a big mystery, an elaborate puzzle you have to solve in order to beat him. Sometimes it's a very well-disguised puzzle, a complex and subtle mystery. Sometimes it's as obvious as a crumbling backhand. But once you unlock that mystery the match is yours. That's what opponent awareness, the third foundation, is all about.

You have to be a private eye out there. You investigate your opponent's game in your scouting, in the warm-up, and during the match, always trying to figure out what his game is. You watch to see how he sits in his chair at the changeover. You watch to see where his ball is landing. You're an investigator.

Once the match begins you should focus most of your concentration on your opponent's court. Instead most players put 90 percent of their concentration on their own game. (How do I feel? Gee, that was a great volley.) That's foolish. You came with the game you've got. And the warm-up is not going to change that. Sure, if your backhand goes off you've got your checkpoints to set you straight, to get you back on course. But the great majority of your concentration should be on your opponent's court. If he does this, I'll do that. If he can't hit a high backhand, I'll hit him a lot of high looping shots to that side. Is he slow? Then I'll run him. Is he tall? Then I'll serve a lot of balls close to his body.

Where is your opponent's vulnerability? What are his

strengths? What part of his game breaks down under pressure? You should study your opponent to find these things out. Become a student of *his* game.

It usually takes a smart player to pick up on a player's weaknesses. For example, when Arthur Ashe beat Jimmy Connors in the 1975 Wimbledon final, he did it with soft puff balls and low stuff to Jimmy's forehand. After that everybody started working on Connors's forehand with low balls. It took Ashe, a thirty-three-year-old veteran who had been strictly a power player throughout his career to show the world how James Scott Connors could be stopped with balls that had little pace.

When a golfer sees a straight and narrow fairway with a dogleg 150 yards away, he doesn't take his driver out and hit the ball 240 yards just because he loves to crack his driver. The same logic applies in tennis. When you meet a certain type of opponent, you don't play a certain way just because that's the way you like to play. You play according to whom you're playing. You adjust your game to beat your opponent. You don't play a run defense against the Denver Broncos even if that's what you're best at because John Elway is going to pass for 450 yards if you do. Likewise don't hit hard against a guy who loves pace.

Many players will hit any old shot they feel like. They've got a big forehand so they'll whack it all over the place no matter what position they or their opponent are in, where it is in the match, or what the score is. You shouldn't hit the ball crosscourt to the opponent's forehand just because it feels good to do it that way. Don't hit what's convenient; hit what's necessary. You've got a job to do if you want to win, and you've got to do it regardless of whether that's the way you *want* to play that day or not. Unless, of course, you like losing.

John McEnroe is loaded with talent. He can hit any shot there is and he even invented a few of his own. But most of what Mac does out there is meant to exploit his opponent. His concentration is almost completely on his opponent's court.

He can hit hard, but the general impression he leaves is that he's toying with his opponent. He messes with his opponent's game, he attacks his rhythm, and he seldom gives the guy a shot he likes to hit.

The fundamentals of hitting the ball are the foundations of your side of the court, which are covered thoroughly in the first part of this book. But learning the foundations of the other side of the court is a key ingredient to becoming a good player. The earlier in your game that you concentrate on what's going on in your opponent's court, the sooner you will really get a complete understanding of tennis. And the sooner you will become a total tennis player.

Why do you think a football coach and his team spend so much time watching game films? They're trying to figure out what their opponents like to do and what they don't like, what their strengths and weaknesses are. They don't just walk out there cold with no game plan and no idea how their opponents play. That would be stupid. Then why do most tennis players constantly walk out on a tennis court with no game plan other than to hit the ball?

Be certain, especially in a tournament, that you know well in advance who you're playing. And if you're serious about winning, if you get mad when you lose, if you destroy your spouse's life for two days after a bad loss, then it's worth the time and effort to scout your opponent.

Many players for some reason think of scouting as if it were spying on the opponent (almost cheating), but scouting is a much-practiced and highly useful method of increasing your understanding of the game. I'm not suggesting that you follow your opponent to his private court and spy on him with binoculars. But why not sit down and closely study a player at your club who you have trouble beating or who you know you're going to play next week in the club championship? He'd probably be flattered.

On the circuit the scrutinizing of other players is a constant pastime. I remember once sitting with Pancho Gonzales while watching Rod Laver play in the late sixties at the Canadian Open. Gonzales said, "Watch Laver's right hip on his serve. When he stops turning his right hip completely, that's when he's tired." Because Laver was not a strong server he tended to tire toward the end of a match on his serve. Sure enough, Laver's hip stayed open and he started serving shorter and then a couple of double faults crept in. And he almost lost the match. Of course, that's a very subtle perception. But often the most obvious observation can be the most effective in developing a good strategy.

I played Jean François Caujolle in 1975 on a fast Laykold court the day after he'd come from playing on the grass at Wimbledon. François was a much better player than I was. (He beat Jimmy Connors in 1980.) I hadn't played circuit tennis for two years, and he was still high in the world rankings. I was clearly outclassed.

There was hope, though. I figured that François had only had that morning to get used to the courts, so I wrote down all the things he'd have trouble adjusting to, all the differences between grass and hard courts. For example, the ball stays very low on grass and the footing is precarious compared to hard courts. In the match I basically did two things: I lofted the ball high and I rushed the net. With the ball up around his shoulders (a ball he hadn't handled in over a month), his returns floated back and I was able to put them away. Also, because of the bad footing on grass, he was accustomed to taking the first volley later, usually behind the service line. On a hard court you can gamble and often get two or three feet inside the service line and still change direction effectively. But on grass if you gamble like that you may slip and be flat on your face. So I stepped in on his service and made him play all my returns early. Here was a guy who without a doubt was twice the player I was, and simply by adjusting two parts of my game I was able to win the match 6–2, 6–2. The only reason I won was that I took the time to analyze my opponent.

You have to scout your opponent. Now sometimes you can run into the problem of an unscouted opponent in the first round of a tournament. But usually someone has seen him play, and if you ask the right questions you'll get a pretty good idea of how to play him.

So what do you look for? What questions do you ask when scouting an opponent? Look first for the direction he hits his shots, particularly the return of serve. Do they go down the line or crosscourt, or does he keep the ball in the middle of the court? Where does he prefer to hit his passing shots? Crosscourt or down the line? Does he lob? When does he lob? Does he change pace? Does he double-fault long or into the net? Also, watch closely for what your opponent does on important points when the pressure is on. Definite patterns usually emerge under pressure because that's when a player almost always goes for the shot he can depend on. Club players are particularly obvious in these situations because they have very few shots that they really have confidence in. On the big points they go for the same shot time after time.

TAKING NOTES

Closely related to scouting is note taking. Tennis is a complex game because every opponent is different, every court is different, every time of day presents different problems. There are so many variables in tennis that it becomes nearly impossible for the mind to juggle all this information and come up with the right piece of information at the right time unless you have some written system for remembering.

Carry a little notebook in your tennis bag, or if you plan to someday play extensive tournament tennis, use index cards you can shuffle and file. But no matter how you take your notes, you'll begin to notice patterns developing, things you do over and over again. These are usually your weaknesses, and simply by jotting down your problems you can begin to see where you need to improve. This one technique alone, note taking, without extra practice or getting in shape or buying a new rocket-powered racquet, will make you a better tennis player because it will help you understand your game better.

Basically, you should take notes on two types of information:

1. General tennis knowledge. Why do volleys have back-spin? How do you vary depth or length or spin? Why and when should you hit a dropshot?

2. Personal observations. How do you react in different match situations? How do your opponents react? Are you stronger in the earlier or later stages of a match? Do you thrive or fold when there is a pressure point? Does competition excite you or frighten you?

HAVE A PLAN

In my job as a TV commentator I have the opportunity to interview dozens of players, and the one thing that really surprises me is that very few of the players have a plan regarding how to play their opponent. These are professional players, mind you. They make their living from winning. It's not just having fun on a weekend at the club. So much depends on their success, and yet they don't bother to scout their opponent to prepare for their matches.

Many players show up at the court with no idea at all how they will play their opponent. How many times have you heard someone say after he's already played a set and a half, "Oh, you're left-handed. That's the problem!" Most players are unaware of the most obvious things. The most important strategy, whether you're a beginner or a touring pro, is that you have a strategy.

A football team prepares all week for a game. They study the opposing team and work out every detail of their game plan. But in tennis it's amazing how many players arrive at the court without the vaguest notion what their strategy will be that day. The most effective strategy is made before the match begins, because there's not much time for thinking during a point. Once you're under pressure there's not much real strategy; it's mostly reactions.

At most levels, most of the time, the most important strategy is preparation—knowing what you're going to do according to the elements involved that day (Are you playing on a clay or hard court? At sea level or in the mountains? At high noon or under lights? During a small hurricane or indoors?), and knowing who your opponent is (Does he play left-handed or two-handed? Is he a ground-stroker or a volleyer? Is he a hard hitter or a touch player?).

You should have a primary game plan and then a second game plan, because even if you've rightly assessed your opponent's weaknesses, he may be better that day or you may not be able to play up to your normal game. The player who has several back-up game plans to use if he sees the match turning against him is the player who will win most often.

YOUR LIMITATIONS AND CAPABILITIES

The important thing about a game plan, however, is that you set up a strategy according to your own ability and your opponent's weaknesses. Some tennis experts said you could overpower McEnroe. But there have only been a few players in the world who could do it. And they better be on that day too. If the average tour player tries that strategy on Mac, John will force him into one error after another.

Don't try to do what you're not capable of doing. In other words, don't use a strategy you can't execute. When most players are told they should change a losing game, they automatically assume that means they have to take pace off the ball. But if you don't have the ability to do that, don't try it.

The basic premise of good strategy, then, is to know your limitations. So many times you'll see a player attempt a shot he has no business trying. Tactics are useless unless you are capable of hitting the shots. Therefore, you must develop an awareness of what you can do and then be realistic about it. Players often have aspirations to attain a level that is totally unrealistic, and as a result they experience a lot of frustration. And when you're frustrated you're not progressing.

It's also important to understand that your limitations and capabilities change from day to day. Some days you've got all your weapons and some days you don't. There are mornings when you bounce out of bed and mornings when it is absolute agony to get up. Or what if you just got a traffic ticket on your way to the match, or you had a fight with your wife, or you lost your life savings because gold went back down to thirty-five dollars an ounce? I can't recall having played even five matches when every element—the weather, the crowd, and my game—was perfect. About 99.9 percent of the times that I've stepped on the court something was wrong.

The player who thinks he can win only when he's got all his weapons, when he's playing his best, will almost never win.

Often a player will go out on the court and if he can't hit all his strokes that day, he throws in the towel. He can't win. He judges his game by his best day and tries to live up to that standard, which is unrealistic. Those perfect days when everything is on come about once in a year.

It takes an extremely intelligent and mature person to get the most out of his game at every moment. If you're not executing your normal shots, you must have the intelligence and courage to change your game and adjust your strategy. You know you're a good player when your game falls apart and you can still win the match.

There are two basic guidelines for assessing your limitations and capabilities. First, match assessment. If you try to maneuver a guy around the court and you just can't get your dropshot to clear the net, that's a limitation. If you're tired, don't try to serve aces. If you have a leg injury, avoid a running game. Second, practice sessions are the time to assess your general overall limitations and capabilities. In other words, practice is when you should try to understand where your game is generally. If you know, for example, before you go out for a match that you can't hit a topspin backhand passing shot down the line, you won't try it.

Specific areas for assessment of your limitations and capabilities include:

1. How mobile are you? Do you have the ability to change direction easily? Are your reactions quick? How is your overall foot speed?

2. Can you hit the ball in any direction—crosscourt and down the line?

3. How fully have you mastered placements? Can you hit the seven target zones?

4. How well can you hit spins (backspin, topspin, and sidespin)?

5. Do you have confidence in your second serve?

6. Can you place your first serve where you want it to go?

WARM-UP

Contrary to how most club players treat the warm-up, it is not the time to practice your strokes. If you don't have the strokes when you arrive for the match, a ten-minute warm-up won't improve them. Instead, the warm-up should be a period of observation of your opponent, not a time to get your game together.

So don't focus your attention on yourself; focus on the person you're playing.

The warm-up should be your chance to sense what's going on with your opponent. Ideally, you've done your scouting so you have a good idea what's going to happen. The warm-up is now a chance to hit with the person and see if you've made the right assessment.

There are times when you can't scout your opponent, however, and the warm-up and the first few games of the match become critical. By the third or fourth game you should have a pretty good handle on what your game plan is. Play the first few games conservatively and see if a pattern develops.

In 1968 I played Wilhelm Bungert. He had made it to the semis at Wimbledon, and he was a very fine and intelligent player. In the warm-up he hit a couple of shots to my forehand, which was my weaker side at the time, and he spotted that weakness immediately. The rest of the warm-up he hit to my backhand. When the match started he never hit me another backhand. Even if he had a setup he wouldn't hit it there. Nothing but forehands. He beat me 6–1, 6–2. It was a horrible experience for me. He just destroyed my game and my confidence for months afterward. He proved to me I couldn't hit a forehand and it was devastating. And all because he read my game before the match started.

Try to start any warm-up at the net; it's the perfect place from which to analyze the other player. He will usually go through his entire repertoire of shots while you volley. It also gives you a chance to read your opponent with on unobstructed view. Up close and personal.

Second, it's easier for you to start warming up at the net because all you have to do is stick your racquet out. The volley is all contact. You don't have to take a big windup to hit the ball, so you're building confidence for the match. Finally, you won't give your opponent the chance to get any rhythm on his ground strokes. With an opposing player at the net most people will hit the ball harder and that throws off their timing. It doesn't give them a chance to establish any feel or rhythm that day.

Hit your opponent different speeds and different spins to see how he handles them. Generally, look for his mood. Is he confident or tentative? Then see how he handles different speeds. He may hate a slow ball and eat up pace, or, conversely, you may be able to overpower him.

Other more specific things to look for:

1. If his lead heel (for a right-handed player the left heel on a forehand, the right heel on a backhand) is planted, it usually means he has confidence in that side.

2. The farther over he steps (the more closed his stance), the more prone he is to go down the line; the more open his stance, the more prone he is to go crosscourt.

3. If his racquet is always open as he takes it back on the backhand, he'll probably float his backhand passing shot under pressure, particularly if the approach is hit without much pace.

4. If he hits with a Continental grip, he's vulnerable to high balls on the forehand.

If you suspect your opponent lacks confidence on his ground strokes, check out his lead heel. If the lead heel is coming off the ground as he hits the ball, it shows he lacks confidence in that stroke. If his lead heel is firmly down, he'll usually hit that shot comfortably.

You can also use different strategies in the warm-up. You can play totally to your opponent's strength or totally to his weakness. If you play to his strength, he'll gain confidence in the warm-up, then as soon as you go to his weakness in the match it may fall apart because it's not warm. Or, if you go to his weakness in the warm-up and then play to his strength immediately in the match, his strength will sometimes break down. (An important point, of course, is to warm up all your own strokes.) Also, if a player needs a lot of rhythm, don't give him any in the warm-up. Hit the ball as hard as you can. Then, when the game starts, give him nothing but puff balls, chips, and dinks.

Finally, play well in the warm-up. It can be a big psychological advantage—often a match is over midway through the warm-up. That's why I've always gone out and hit for an hour or so right up until I have to play. Have the groove, be physically and mentally sharp in a warm-up. Make very few mistakes and you'll put a lot of pressure on your opponent. One final tip is to hit every ball on one bounce or in the air as a volley in the warm-up. This will prepare you for the real energy level of the match.

PREMATCH HITTING

Don't confuse the warm-up with your prematch hitting. The warm-up is to find out about your opponent. The prematch session is to get your own game feeling right and to find out what you've got that day. If you find you have a big serve but shaky forehand that day, it will influence your strategy and how you approach your warm-up.

Use the prematch hitting to get ready, to get used to the court surface, the balls, the general weather conditions that day.

Your feel that day is directly related to how you warm up. The ideal way to warm up is to hit the ball normally for the first two or three minutes. Hit a lot of different shots to check out what you've got. In other words, scout your own game. Then focus in on your problems. Are you having trouble with timing? Is your accuracy off? Are your touch shots off?

Also, prepare yourself according to who you're going to play that day, whether it's a baseliner or a serve-and-volleyer, a hard hitter or a dinker. A few years ago I was scheduled to meet Colin Dibley in a match in the thirty-five and over division at the United States Open. Now Colin has a serve clocked in excess of 140 miles per hour. So I had a friend serve to me from his service line. When I got out on the court and faced Colin's serve, it actually looked relatively slow and I ended up breaking Colin seven times in the match. Unfortunately, I forgot to warm up my own serve, and Dibley broke me nine times to win the match.

STRENGTHS AND WEAKNESSES, LIKES AND DISLIKES

Everyone has his likes and dislikes on the tennis court—his favorite shot, his most comfortable position, the speed he likes to hit the ball. There isn't a player in the world who likes to serve and volley and hit ground strokes equally well. Or a guy who likes to take the ball at any height and any speed. Everyone has a preference.

There's a whole bunch of pro players who skyrocketed up the rankings when they first came on the tour. Then they ran into some smart players who figured out how to exploit their weaknesses. Soon the word got out and down the rankings they went. The players on the pro tour don't just step aside for the hot newcomer. They look for something he doesn't like and when they find it, they feed it to him until he chokes.

In a warm-up you are trying to decide what your opponent's strengths and weaknesses are. You can tell that by his likes and dislikes. And that's easy to find out because he'll tell you what he's most comfortable with right away. Just hit the first ball in warm-up down the middle right at him, and he'll step to one side or the other and take the ball on his forehand or backhand. This little bit of investigative work almost never fails. Think about it. What shot do you take when you first walk out on the court? Whatever you're most comfortable with, of course. And that, inevitably, is your stronger side. A player's likes and dislikes depend on what his strengths are. Very rarely do you see a player who likes to come to the net if he's lousy up there.

You can tell what a player likes to do by the shots he always takes. It's that easy. For example, most women players around the country at the C and B levels stand at the baseline and bang balls at each other. No dropshots. No angles. Nothing but hitting the ball back. They seldom come to the net—even in a warm-up—so you can be absolutely sure they hate to volley. Another typical situation is the guy who never takes overheads in his warm-up. He may pretend that his overhead is so devastating he doesn't need to warm it up, but you can bet it's because he doesn't have one.

As soon as you've determined what your opponent doesn't like, proceed to make him unhappy.

THE TWO OPPOSITES

Every player has areas of weakness and strength and preference. I guarantee you that no player will do all things well: Most players think attacking your opponent means hitting harder and running faster. But attacking is merely the exploitation of his or her weaknesses. And the greatest tool for exploiting your opponent is the utilization of the two opposites. There is a pair of opposites for every facet of tennis. The trick is to find the one with which your opponent has trouble. Forehand or backhand? Volleys or ground strokes? High shots or low? Hard or soft? Shots hit wide or right at him? Making him run for every ball or giving him all day to hit a shot?

Divide the court into the deuce and ad courts and ask, is he stronger on the backhand or the forehand? Then check his movement. Does he move better laterally or up and back? In other words, pick his game apart.

In the beginning you will generalize. "Well, my opponent can't hit a second serve," you might say. But the more sophisticated you get in reading your opponent, the more you will be able to particularize that person's weaknesses. For example, he may have a great low forehand but have real trouble with a high ball. Or he may have a good backhand until you pressure him on that side.

A common pattern, in fact, is a player who likes a hard ball to his forehand and a soft ball to his backhand. So a frequently used tactic is to hit a slow ball to the forehand and blast everything to his backhand.

A high ball to the backhand is usually a tough shot for any player at any level, except if the opponent has a two-handed backhand. Then they usually love a high ball to the backhand. A low ball, however, drives the two-hander crazy.

The same thing applies to the volley. Test out all the combinations—high and low, hard and soft, backhand and forehand. Now, a player may have a solid volley in all these areas, but in a rapid-fire volley exchange at the net they may have trouble reacting.

Another thing to remember is that sometimes you will try something and it will work for a while and then your opponent will catch on to it. His weakness can become his strength by the second set. So the smart player often stays away from his opponent's weakness early and goes to it at, say, 40–30. He exploits his weakness on the important points. Why go to his weakness at 40–0 when you can win the game going at his strength?

Another common weakness is poor fitness. There are players who are very good ground-strokers. They can bang winners from anywhere on the court and love pressure—the tighter the match the more accurate they become. But they may be out of shape. A player like that will often win by scores like 6–0, 7–5. He always annihilates his opponent in the first set and almost never wins a three-setter. In other words, his strokes and his effectiveness diminish as the match goes on. This is not uncommon. In fact, nearly everyone's strokes worsen with fatigue. It's natural. As the body tires, nerves and muscles and major organs don't function as well. A player who cracks aces in the first two or three games may not be able to keep it up for two or three sets. That's what makes Boris Becker's serve so great. It's not the fastest ever (though it's very nearly the fastest) but he can still blast it 120 miles per hour in the fifth set. Not many other players today can do that.

If you know or suspect an opponent is out of shape (his lack of mobility or a prodigious beer gut are pretty good indications), then run him for three or four games and see how he holds up.

He may win the first four games and then fold and never hit another decent shot all day.

Bobby Riggs, winner of several senior grand slams (the national grass, clay, hard, and indoor championships in an age division) told me that when he plays a match on the senior circuit he doesn't care who wins the first set. His only thought is to wear down his opponent. A typical Riggs score is 4–6, 6–2, 6–0. When you're playing an opponent who's through for the day and there are still two sets to go, the match is yours.

If you suspect an opponent is out of shape, test him. If he fails the test he will probably never beat you again. At least, until he shapes up.

BUSTING STRENGTHS

Most strategy involves finding an opponent's strength and then denying him the chance to use it. The only exception is when you decide to bust your opponent's strength. The basic theory is to put so much pressure on your opponent's best shots that those strengths fold, and then his confidence goes and with that his entire game crumbles.

There's more to busting a strength than simply pounding the ball at your opponent's forehand. The key is the utilization of the two opposites. If a player has a big forehand it's usually big in a certain way. He either hits it flat or with topspin, or he's got great direction or great pace or disguise. Very few players have a strength that is perfect in every way.

If your opponent has a great forehand, start with backspins, then throw in topspins, make him run, or float the ball at him. See if he can handle them all. Also, a player with a strong shot usually has rhythm, so give him dropshots, side-T placements, and chip shots. If you get him out of his groove, he may begin to suspect his best weapon isn't all that potent.

Steffi Graf has the most potent forehand in women's tennis today. Yet Martina Navratilova plays to Graf's forehand a lot. Against Martina, Steffi doesn't see a lot of backhands early in the match. So it forces her into the center of the court. Then Martina starts working over Graf's backhand with the approach shot.

Every other player is so scared of Graf's forehand that they try to hit every shot into her backhand, so she cheats over to that side and is waiting to hit her forehand. And from that position she's got the whole court open to her. She can drive the ball down the line or hit that deadly inside-out forehand crosscourt to the opponent's backhand.

The problem for Martina is that now Graf's backhand is

nearly as strong as her forehand, so the tactic is working less and less well as time goes by.

Some players' greatest asset is their legs. Because a player who depends on his speed will usually try to move before the ball is hit, when playing against a good runner try to hit the ball back to the spot where he just came from. He'll break for the open court before you hit the ball, which, of course, leaves that part of the court open.

Another way to counter a runner is to hit down the center, because a runner will usually hit the ball better on the move. He's running so much he doesn't know what it's like to hit standing still. Again, give the opponent what he doesn't like.

Remember, just as your own game changes from day to day, so does your opponent's. Look for signs that his best shot is not quite as strong that day.

CHANGING YOUR GAME

If you've been paying attention at all, it's probably pretty obvious to you that to be a good player you've got to be willing to change your game according to who you're playing. You've got to be flexible. You have to play differently against different opponents.

You also have to be willing to change your game when you start losing. If you've been chipping at a net-charging server and he suddenly starts to stay back, your tactic may backfire on you if you keep it up.

The ability to change your game to suit the opponent and the situation may, in fact, be the most important quality of a good tennis player. And it's a sure sign that he has built a total game and a complete understanding of tennis.

Sometimes a change can mean simply elevating your level of concentration. That's the first thing you have to determine. Are you just playing lousy, or do you have to change your game? You have to be honest with yourself. There are too many players in a state of total illusion when it comes to their game. Some players just don't know what to do when things go wrong because they're not sure what's happening. They can't see how poorly they're playing and how well their opponent is playing.

Sometimes you meet a guy who's in the zone and you've got to recognize that fact and adjust accordingly. Most players figure they're just not playing well when the reality is their opponent is making them hit tough shots or he's hitting winners from all over the court. They think he's just lucky. You've got to accept the fact the guy is good or he's at least having a good day.

Maybe the most important part of changing your game is

knowing when to do it. If it's 5–4 in the first set and you're playing pretty darn good, don't change. That's the time to put your energy and concentration into high gear, not to bail out. The exception to this rule is if you've had a very long first set and it's still only 3–3 and you're not in shape to stay out there for two or three hours. Then it's probably a good time to pick up the pace of the match. Try to end the points sooner.

It's also important to know the difference between a change in the level of your opponent's play and a couple of lucky shots. A player will hit two close-your-eyes winners off your serve and you find yourself down 0–30. So you stay back, which is exactly what he was hoping for. The momentum has shifted because you failed to realize he got lucky.

When should you change? When you're in a losing pattern. If you've been broken twice and you can see the match slipping away, look for a way to upset the momentum of the match. Usually, you won't change after the first break because a break can come off a couple of untimely let cords. Something lucky. Of course, if you go out there and your opponent rifles four returns by you, you might get the idea that your serve just isn't strong enough against this guy to come to the net.

If you make a change you must do so before the first set is over. That is critical. If you lost the fifth game of the first set to go down 4–1, it's time to change, especially if he's serving for 5–1. A lot of players will wait until it's 6–1, 2–0, and that's just too late to stop the momentum. If you're in the first set, you're really in trouble, and you know if you continue to play the way you're playing and your opponent continues the way he's playing it's going to be over, that's the time to make a change.

CHAPTER 17

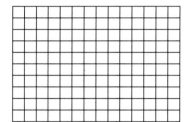

PLAYER TYPES

LEFTIES

How many times have you heard a player say, "I was into the second set before I realized I was playing a left-hander." The first step in handling a left-hander is to know you're playing one. The second step is getting used to him. Rod Laver lost to a number of lefties he faced in the late sixties because prior to that time he had played approximately five years in a closed pro circuit in which there were no other left-handers.

Watch next time you see a guy play a lefty and notice how often he'll serve and volley to his forehand. It's programmed. You must almost retrain yourself to play a lefty. That's why it's good to practice with a left-handed player whenever possible.

There are two main problems when playing a left-hander. First of all, the ball is spinning oddly when it comes toward you because a lefty puts spin on the ball from a different side. A lefty's topspin forehand will tend to curve into a right-hander's forehand, and his backspin backhand will spin away from the righty's backhand. The only strategy to counter a lefty's spin is to be prepared.

The second main problem when playing a lefty is where you hit the ball—in particular, trying to hit to his backhand side. Your normal approach to a right-hander's vulnerable backhand plays right into a lefty's booming forehand. Another difficult adjustment is hitting backhand volleys down the line, which is not an easy shot. It's a shot you hit against a right-hander only about 20 percent of the time (because you're hitting to his fore-hand), but suddenly against a lefty you must hit your backhand there about 80 percent of the time. Even if you miss that shot only two or three times in a match, that might be enough to lose to a player you should beat.

Unless you can hit a good slice, serving to a lefty's backhand can be difficult. If you're having problems try standing two or three feet from the center line when serving to the deuce court. In the ad court get as close to the center line as possible.

A significant area of weakness for lefties is the low forehand volley. In New Zealand one time Tony Roche (himself a lefty) told me that lefties have trouble with that shot because a lefty's slice serve to the ad court forces a right-hander to hit most of his returns down the line to a lefty's backhand volley. Therefore, lefties see very few forehand volleys and it naturally becomes a weakness.

TWO-HANDERS

There is a dangerous species roaming the court in greater numbers these days—the two-hander. There have always been two-handed players in tennis (Pancho Segura, remember, had a two-handed *forehand*). But since Connors and Evert's great success with the two-handed backhand, this shot is seeing its greatest popularity.

The two-hander is a young person's shot. It provides extra strength to weak wrists and arms, but it also requires greater physical exertion. Because of the limitations of reach, a two-handed player must take an extra step or two to hit the ball well. With a one-handed shot, if you're stretched out, you can still get off a decent shot even though your arm is fully extended. But to supply any force at all a two-handed shot must be hit with the arms bent. All those extra steps add up to 30 to 40 percent more running. So, to hit a two-handed shot effectively you'd better be in top physical shape—which usually means young.

To beat a two-hander, then, make him stretch for shots. Use the side T's to run him wide, and unless he's very quick and extremely fit, he'll be an old man by the second set.

Two-handers also don't like slow backspin shots. Pam Shriver was 0–16 against Evert, but finally beat her for the first time by hitting Chris lots of slow underspin shots to her backhand. Backspin keeps the ball low and forces two-handers out of their left-hand–dominant shot. As long as the ball is high they can keep their left hand in a locked position, which they need to do in order to gain leverage. The low soft shot forces them to drop the racquet head down and their wrist goes into a weaker position. They then have trouble doing anything with the ball.

Another effective strategy is to hit the ball high and directly

One of the major weak-
nesses of a two-handed
ground stroke is its limited
reach.

A two-handed player often
must release her top hand
to get to low balls, which
is why I always encourage
players who use two
hands to also learn a one-
handed backhand.

Another disadvantage of
the two-handed backhand
occurs when the ball is hit
hard directly at you.

at the two-hander, because the left hand on the racquet inhibits
the movement of both his arms toward the right side of his body.
This shot is especially effective when the two-hander is in a
emergency situation and has no time to move and take the ball
on his forehand.

Two-handers are topspin players. Very few hit two-handed
backspin or even a forehand backspin for that matter. So they
very seldom have good dropshots or volleys or defensive lobs
—any shot, in fact, that requires backspin. This is a crucial
weakness that severely limits their game.

Perhaps a two-hander's greatest weakness, however, is a low
volley. A two-hander usually holds the racquet with two Eastern
or semi-Western forehands, and therefore to open the face of
the racquet in order to volley a low ball upward, the wrists must
turn into an awkward position. The first thing I do when I get
a two-hander as a student is to teach him how to volley one-
handed with a Continental grip, because to volley with a Western
or Eastern forehand, even with the support of two hands, is a
very difficult task. So when you play a two-hander, see if he
volleys with two hands on the backhand. If he does, force him
to hit a lot of low volleys.

SPIN ARTISTS

When a ball is spinning it will alter its normal course when it lands—either bounce higher or lower, to the left or right. When the ball has the potential to alter course it means many times you aren't able to predict what it will do. That's an emergency, so against a spin artist, shorten your backswing. Don't try to overpower a spin artist—try to outmaneuver him.

Also, try to bring a spin artist to the net, because he usually hates the net. A spin artist usually doesn't have great volleys or overheads—he just tries to get the ball back in. In fact, he seldom has power in any stroke, so he has developed his spin game to compensate for his lack of strength. Of course, there are players who can hit softly and hard, blast it or finesse it. If you meet a player like that, I offer my sympathies.

THE HEAVY-TOPSPIN PLAYER

Unlike the spin artist, the heavy-topspin player is a power player. He seldom hits a touch shot or even cares to.

The first rule when playing a heavy-topspin player is to counteract heavy spin with more spin. Chip him to death. Keep the ball low with lots of underspin and the heavy top-spinners will usually start to mishit.

Jimmy Arias is a typical topspin player, and he doesn't like to hit a wide backhand because he likes the ball in tight so he can roll his hand over the top of the ball. Balls short and wide with lots of backspin drive him nuts.

If you feel confident enough to come back at a topspinner with heavy topspin of your own, hit it back that way as a change of pace or if you feel you can simply overpower his power. But when it comes to your backhand, you'll probably want to hit it back with underspin.

Also, a good idea is to jam a heavy top-spinner. He usually likes to take a big looping backswing so if you hit the ball right at him, he'll often hit a weaker shot as he steps back away from it.

THE BLASTER

The opposite of the spin artist is the blaster—the guy who has to hit every ball as hard as he can. A good player will not use this strategy, so this is usually an intermediate or beginning player. A big ego and total lack of understanding of the game are his chief trademarks.

A blaster usually wins because he bores you to death. You may or may not hit a solid ball all day. To beat him, hang tight. That is, squeeze tight on the racquet with the bottom three fingers so the racquet doesn't fly out of your hand and utilize minimum potential. Just block everything back. Don't try to hit harder than he does even if he calls you a sissy because you won't "hit like a man." Just play your game.

After you beat him several times, he'll go back to karate.

CHAPTER 18

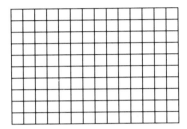

ANTICIPATION AND DISGUISE

YOUR OPPONENT IS AN OPEN BOOK
WAITING TO BE READ

Once that ball leaves your racquet you should be thinking solely about what the ball is doing in your opponent's court and what and where your opponent's next shot will be.

Joakim Nystrom was asked how he was able to break Becker's serve so frequently. "Well," he said, "he tells me where he's going to serve it all the time." And Becker is actually pretty difficult to read. If I had to pick one player in the world whose serve is well disguised, I'd have to say Becker. But if he is giving away his serve to a trained eye, imagine how easy it would be to read other players' shots.

Reading your opponent is a basic principle of all sport. The moment film was created some football coach used it to scout his opponents. Teams spend their whole week pondering their opponent's previous games—what they do when they line up this way, the subtleties that tip off that play. They watch the quarterback closely. If he's going to pass, he may lean back from the center before the snap. If it's a running play, he's hunched more closely over the center as he takes the snap.

This is known as anticipation, and it has always been considered a very advanced bit of tennis knowledge. But I teach anticipation to beginners almost immediately. Now, I'm not talking about a high level of sophistication at the start. I'm talking about very simple basics. As you get better the level of sophistication gets higher and higher until you can see by the subtlest positions and movements of an opponent's body what he's going to do before he does it.

In all other sports disguise is taught right from the beginning. That's why they have a huddle in football and signals in baseball. And why when they line up at the line of scrimmage, they do it so they won't tip off the opponent as to what's coming. The opponents have likewise spent hours in the film room prior to the game trying to figure out what you're likely to do next.

Primarily, anticipation is the ability to have a reasonably good idea where your opponent's shot is going before he hits it. But anticipation is also determining what the ball will do in terms of its spin and height, getting off the mark on time, and positioning yourself according to what you believe will happen.

The first prerequisite of being a private investigator out on the court is to free yourself from watching the ball all the time. If you don't, you're not going to be able to see what your opponent is up to. Reading your opponent is an art. You must train your eye to really see what's going on out there on the court, and you should learn to do this early in your career.

Triple vision is the whole foundation of anticipation and reading your opponent. If you're not anticipating and reading your opponent, it means your focus is not on his court. And if your focus is not on your opponent, *you will never be a good tennis player*.

READING YOUR OPPONENT'S RACQUET

Ultimately, the ball is going to do what the racquet makes it do. So if you understand what happens to the ball when the opponent's racquet face does certain things, you'll be developing anticipation.

First, you should be aware of how your opponent is setting up his racquet—whether he's taking a big backswing, a medium backswing, or no backswing, and whether the face is open or closed. For example, if his racquet face is open just prior to contact it will probably be a backspin shot and you'll know the ball is going to bounce low, travel a little more slowly, and, perhaps, float. Secondly, be aware of what his racquet does after contacting the ball. If his racquet finishes high and on edge, chances are it will be a topspin shot; if his racquet finishes at the same level or lower than where he contacted the ball and the strings point to the sky, it's sure to be a backspin shot.

Have you ever seen a home-run hitter in baseball? He puts his whole body into the swing. If you see your opponent take a big windup, you can be very sure he's going to try to wallop that ball. Expect trouble. If your opponent is off balance or takes a short backswing and a weak swing at the ball, expect a softer, slower ball.

Learning to read your opponent is not as difficult as it sounds. For example, you can see here that the player's backswing is very short and chances are he's going to hit a soft shot or even a dropshot. A big backswing usually indicates the player will hit the ball hard.

By watching your opponent's racquet preparation, you can usually determine what type of spin he's going to hit. For example, the player here takes his racquet back low and with a closed racquet face. He will most likely hit topspin since most topspin shots are hit with a low-to-high swing and a closed racquet face.

On the other hand, here the player prepares with a high backswing and an open racquet face and most likely will hit a backspin shot.

163

If your opponent drops his racquet head early he is probably going to lob.

THE FRAME OF CONCENTRATION

Zero in not on the ball, but on where the ball can possibly go. If the ball is going to stay in the court, the ball is only going to come off the racquet in a very small area or "window." Your frame of concentration should focus on that window. Everything else is an out ball. When a player sets up for underspin, watch for the trajectory of the ball. The height it comes off the racquet is the tip. If you're at the net and you see the ball coming low, you move in. If you see it coming off high, you move back for the deeper ball.

The human body is a machine. There are some major signals the body gives if it's going to do something a certain way. Different parts do different things. The shoulder and hips turn a certain way when you're going to hit the ball in a particular direction. For example, when a player is going to hit the ball down the line on his backhand, the shoulder turn will often be so pronounced you can almost see his back. The positioning of the legs and feet will also tell you a lot. If a player steps with his front foot across his body, he's almost certain to hit the ball down the line.

As you get better at reading people's games, your eye will get more subtle and you'll begin to read the small body movements such as the wrist or the grip or the slight lifting of the front heel that shows a lack of confidence on ground strokes.

The volley can be read mostly by shoulder turn. When an opponent is going down the line, his lead shoulder is more closed. When he's going to hit the ball crosscourt, the lead shoulder opens up prematurely. The more subtle tip-off is the wrist. When he's going down the line, he will lay the wrist back so the racquet is about perpendicular to the court. When he's going to go crosscourt, he'll keep it cocked with the racquet head up.

ANTICIPATION AND YOUR OPPONENT'S POSITION

Anticipation is linked to the word *limitation*. Your opponent may be limited to one or two possible shots by his position on the court. In other words, the better shot you hit, the more limited your opponent is. If you hit a great shot his only return will probably be a lob. A deep approach to his backhand will severely limit your opponent's shot selection, and if you know he has trouble going crosscourt you've limited him further. Or, if your opponent is three feet from the net and the ball lands low at his feet, you know quite a number of things. For example, he can't hit it hard, and in order to clear the net he must put an arc on the ball, which means the ball will probably sit up nicely for you.

MATCH MEMORY

Anticipation is simply a matter of reading your opponent. And that implies not just reading him at that moment, but knowing what he likes to do, what his preference is, and what he's liable to do in certain situations.

A good investigator is like a good card player. He remembers the cards the opponent has played. Players develop patterns both physically and strategically. They will hit a particular shot when they are in a certain place on the court or in a certain match situation, or when they set up a certain way. When those big points arrive at, say, 4–5, 30–40, or in a tiebreaker; if you remember what your opponent likes to do, you've got a huge advantage. For example, when they're in trouble most players hit their backhand passing shots down the line. Or, if it's match point and you come to the net, they may lob every time.

Take Tim Mayotte. He is a very patterned player. It's one of his few weaknesses. He will do the same thing time after time in a certain way in a certain situation. Most players know what's coming from Tim. He is not a creative player, so he is truly an open book. If he adds creativity to his repertoire, he's got the potential to be very dangerous.

It is also vitally important to be able to read when an opponent is falling apart. The sooner you can pick out what's gone wrong, the sooner you can really put the pressure on your opponent. This can be as obvious a thing as fatigue. When you see a guy resting with his hands on his knees between points, it's obviously a good time to pick up the tempo of the match and begin to move him around. Another tip-off of a crumbling opponent is a player who drastically changes the pattern of his game for no good reason. For example, he may hit a lot of topspin and then inexplicably start to hit nothing but underspin. Suddenly, he's scared and tentative. So it's time to attack.

DISGUISE

Disguise and anticipation are inseparable because reading disguise *is* anticipation. In order to understand your opponent's racquet you must understand your own. Basically, disguise is being able to do everything the same on every shot right up until the moment of contact. If you use the same racquet preparation on every shot, then you'll be learning disguise. And as you progress as a player, this becomes more and more significant.

Disguise, like anticipation, has also been considered a very advanced technique. But I teach disguise in the first year, because the whole concept of my teaching is to instruct the beginner the same way as the advanced player. However, I teach the beginner simple disguise—not so much to disguise his own shots as to read disguise, so he'll know, for example, that when his opponent's racquet head drops down low it's probably going to be a lob.

If you toss a particular way for a particular serve the intelligent returner will know what's coming. The old way of teaching the serve was to toss the ball right for a spin serve, straight ahead for flat, and back over the head for topspin. All you're doing is tipping off the receiver.

Also, if you set up for a ground stroke a certain way every time, you're giving away what's coming. If you always take your racquet way back to hit power shots and you use almost no backswing for a drop shot, you're tipping your hand. If you point your foot down the line when you intend to hit that way, you're telling the opponent where you're going to hit the ball. Your goal should be to try to set your racquet and body and feet up the same way each time. That's disguise!

PART III
TIME, PLACE, AND CIRCUMSTANCE:
WHEN AND WHERE TO HIT WHAT
TO WHOM

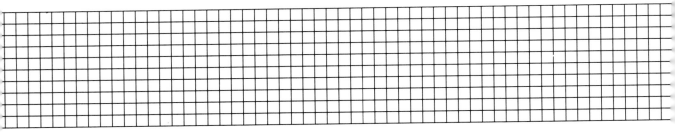

CHAPTER 19

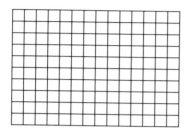 PERCENTAGE TENNIS

PRIORITIES VERSUS PERCENTAGES

I don't stress percentages because I don't really think people understand them. In fact, a great majority of the time they do not make sense. For example, if the percentage suggests a down-the-line approach to the opponent's backhand and the opponent has the greatest backhand since Don Budge, is that a high-percentage shot?

There are books that plot out exactly the percentage of times you should hit your serves, ground strokes, and volleys to a certain spot. But that approach is extremely misleading, because percentages change according to the circumstances, who your opponent is, and where and when the match is played. Where and when you hit each shot is determined much more by priorities than percentages.

Priorities take precedence, and your priority is to go to your opponent's vulnerabilities, to his weaknesses. If your opponent doesn't have any vulnerabilities you can exploit over and over, then you play the percentages. If you can't exploit your opponent through priorities or percentages, you've got a tough match on your hands.

Still, your overall game plan is determined by priorities. For example, if your opponent has a weak forehand, your priority is to exploit it. Every time you play someone different, you have a different game plan—so the percentages change each time. What may be a high-percentage shot against one player is suicide against another. According to traditional percentage strategy, for example, you should serve to the backhand 80 percent of the time. But if your opponent can't return your slice serve to the deuce court, then, of course, you should slice a lot to his forehand.

You always have two or three possibilities for strategy in a match, and the success of a good tennis player depends on his ability to select and place those possibilities according to priority. For example, if you're playing an opponent who is pretty vulnerable on one side, but it's a very swirling, windy day, you can no longer think about playing to his weakness. Your priority is trying to figure out which direction the wind is blowing and how you can get the ball to land somewhere in the court. On a very hot day your priority may be different than on a cool day. Instead of serving and volleying, you may want to save your energy and try to make your opponent run.

Your own strengths can be your priorities. Forget the opponent if your strength is stronger than his strength. You don't have to worry about percentages at all. Like Steffi Graf and Ivan Lendl, your priority becomes to run around your backhand and crack your forehand every time you possibly can. If, on the other hand, your weakness is weaker then your opponent's weakness, your priority becomes to protect your weakness.

80–20 TENNIS

The basis of playing percentage tennis is relying on the 80–20 formula. The basic reasoning behind 80–20 tennis is that there are particular areas of weakness in almost all players that are generally the same. So there are particular angles and particular shots that should be played most of the time if you want the percentages on your side. For example, if you serve 80 percent of the time to your opponent's backhand, you're probably going to win most of those points. (This presumes, of course, that you are on the same level as your opponent. If you're playing someone who is far superior to you, then the percentages mean very little.)

But most club players often go to that generally weaker side (the backhand) less than 50 percent of the time. They hit it to the opponent's forehand because it feels more comfortable to hit it there.

Don't hit what's convenient or comfortable. Hit what's practical. That's 80–20 tennis. Volleying to your opponent's backhand may not be a particularly comfortable shot. It may feel awkward and you're going to have to move more to get in position for the next shot. Also, a backhand volley down the line is harder to hit than a crosscourt shot. But against a left-hander that's a shot you've got to hit a lot because that's where his backhand is.

Remember one thing, though: you don't want to become obsessed with percentage tennis. Players become so caught up with where they should hit the ball 80 percent of the time that they forget the other 20 percent. They hit the ball to the same spot *every* time. That 20 percent of the time when you go to the other side is very important because it sets up the effectiveness of the 80-percent shot. For instance, good players know you should, under normal circumstances, serve 80 percent of the time to the opponent's backhand. But they'll often go three or four games without hitting any serves to the forehand side. Pretty soon the opponent's backhand is grooved and he's hitting it better than his forehand.

ESTABLISHING SHOTS

Percentage tennis is the basis for establishing certain shots like hitting the first volley to the opponent's backhand corner or serving to his backhand. In other words, let the opponent know that you can hit that shot and that you are going to go there most of the time. When you establish those 80–20 shots, you're finding out if your opponent can play tennis. You're setting up the percentages in your favor. If he can beat those percentages, he's a good player.

On the first volley you have to establish that you will go to your opponent's backhand corner most of the time. If you don't the opponent will always be able to cheat on you. Keep putting the ball in that corner and he has to play that side of the court. That enables you to go to his forehand corner, and he won't be there waiting with his power to attack you. Instead, he'll be leaning into the backhand corner because you've established that shot in his mind.

You also have to establish a slice serve wide to the forehand court to keep the returner off balance. You've got to let him know you can hit that serve. Otherwise, he can get a groove on your serve to the backhand. Or he could even cheat so far over that he can run around his backhand even on first serves. This happens frequently in the deuce court because it's tough for a right-handed server to get the ball into another righty's backhand on that side of the court. And if your opponent knows you can't swing him wide, he can cheat toward the middle.

You also have to establish a dropshot. Your opponent has to at least know you can hit it, or he doesn't have to cover the short corners.

GAMBLING

There are certain times when you should gamble on a low-percentage shot. Just try to hit an outright winner. Players have got to learn when to go for it. At 40–0, go for it.

The most common time you defy percentages, however, is when your opponent is guaranteed to play percentage tennis. At 30–40 very, very few players will gamble. That's when you try to hit a winner. Or against a serve-and-volleyer on your first match point, go for a winner. Try to take the match right there. With his back against the wall he is sure to play a very conservative point and, besides that, if he has a great serve-and-volley game you may never get another chance.

THE LADDER OF DIFFICULTY AND YOUR PERCENTAGES

Playing percentages has a lot to do with your shot selection and climbing the ladder of difficulty. If you can simply outsteady your opponent, why do anything else? That's the lowest rung on the ladder of difficulty. Just get the ball over one more time than your opponent.

Test your opponent. See what he can handle. If he can handle the easy shot, then go to the next level—hit with more spin or put him on the move. If he can handle that, up the game another level.

What Pat Cash can do so well is hit a tougher and tougher volley according to how well his opponent is playing. If he's playing a guy who is just a so-so passer, Cash will hit a nice safe volley into the backhand corner. But if his opponent can really hit ground strokes, Pat will hit a very forcing volley.

That's climbing the ladder of difficulty, raising your game only to the level you need to beat your opponent. If you try the most difficult shots all the time, if you try to graze the line on every passing shot, pretty soon even a mediocre player will be able to give you a tough match because you will be handing him game after game.

UNFORCED ERRORS

Closely related to the ladder of difficulty is unforced errors. The unforced error is one of the most telling statistics when reviewing the outcome of a match, and most unforced errors are the result of poor concentration, or trying a shot for no good reason. For example, if you are on the baseline exchanging groundies with your opponent, you should never make an error into the net because there's no reason to hit the ball low. You should be concentrating on depth and a reasonable three- to five-foot clearance of the net. Any ball hit into the net in a baseline rally is (except for a dropshot) a dumb shot—and, of course, an unforced error.

CHAPTER 20

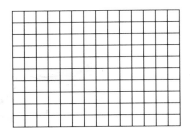

THE STRATEGY FOR
THE RETURN OF SERVE

THE RETURN OF SERVE AND YOUR PERCENTAGES

There is one situation in tennis where percentages become your priority—on the return of serve. When returning a serve you should have some preconceived idea of what you want to do with the ball. For instance, if you're playing a serve-and-volleyer you should hit low returns to his feet. If you're playing a baseliner you should aim for good clearance of the net and good depth.

Percentages concerning the return of serve are important and are based entirely on where the serve is hit.

ON A SERVE TO THE FOREHAND IN THE FOREHAND COURT

If it's a hard serve you should hit 80–90 percent of your returns crosscourt because you should seldom change the direction of a hard-hit ball. It is based on the physics principle that the "angle of incidence equals the angle of reflection." If a ray of light hits a perfectly flat surface, the ray will reflect off at exactly the same angle. In tennis terms, if you hit the ball crosscourt, back where it came from, there is a great deal of room for error even on a fast serve. But if you try to change the ball's direction by going down the line, your timing and the angle of the racquet face must be exact. That's why when a player tries to go down the line in those circumstances the ball often goes way wide. If the serve is soft you can hit 80 percent of your returns down the line to the backhand, but when you're in trouble the best shot is crosscourt. *Note*: For a right-hander, the forehand court is the deuce court. But for a left-hander, the forehand court is the ad court.

ON A SERVE TO THE BACKHAND IN
THE FOREHAND COURT

Regardless of the speed of the serve, return 80 percent down the line. One of the most difficult shots in tennis is trying to return crosscourt off the backhand in the forehand court.

ON A SERVE TO THE FOREHAND IN
THE BACKHAND COURT

If the ball is hit hard, the best percentage is to go down the center. Or if you're really accurate, try to hit to your opponent's backhand side. If it's a softly hit ball, pound it to the opponent's backhand 80 percent of the time. *Note*: For a right-hander, the backhand court is the ad court. But for a left-hander, the backhand court is the deuce court.

ON A SERVE TO THE BACKHAND IN
THE BACKHAND COURT

Return 80 percent crosscourt. If the server tries to make it all the way to the net to cut off your return (by not check stepping at the service line), lob.

Following percentages on the return of serve will get you the best results, but it's your game. If something suits you better, do it! Arthur Ashe approached the return of serve in a different way. He had confidence he'd win his serve every time (and who wouldn't with his delivery), so his plan was to hit the return of serve as hard as he could for the first three or four games to see if he could get a break. It was a low-percentage tactic, but often he'd string together enough winners to get the break and that was all he felt he needed to win a set. If the set got to 4–4, he'd go back to playing the percentages. I don't recommend this tactic, but if you've got Ashe's talent, almost everything works.

HITTING THE RETURN

If you ask most players what the purpose of the return is, a lot of them will reply, "To hit a winner." But they're wrong. The number-one purpose of the return of serve is to neutralize the opponent. You should not be trying to go for a winner on

When returning serve, many players tend to bend too far forward at the waist. Not only is this hard on the lower back, but it tends to limit the player's ability to handle different heights of balls. It's better to bend the knees and keep the back straight. A good way to check for this in practice is to stick a racquet handle down the back of your pants. The racquet head will touch both shoulder blades if you are in balance.

the return of serve. Rather, you should be trying to go from a defensive position to a neutral one.

A junior player will often try to hit a winner on every return of serve. That's Boris Becker's big mistake. He tries to go for it on almost every return. He never really gets into as many points as he should. He generally wins it outright or he loses it outright.

Instead, just let the ball rebound off your racquet strings, and because of the speed of the serve you can hit a very decent return with minimal racquet movement. The great returners have very limited backswings. They are very compact. They don't flail at the ball because the first prerequisite of a good returner is that he gets the ball back consistently.

After you've established a consistent return, start climbing the ladder of difficulty by going through the five dimensions just as you would on ground strokes.

1. *Getting it in.* Handle the return of serve as if it were a volley. The great returners are often great volleyers because the return is really very much like a volley—a short backswing and a limited follow-through. Your concentration is all on contacting the ball. Eliminate a large backswing even on a full-out forehand return meant to produce a winner. Why do you need a big backswing? For extra power. The pace of the serve itself will supply most of the power you'll need. Go back to the basics of contact area and point the strings where you want the ball to go.

2. *Direction.* Whether your opppoonent is serving and volleying or staying back, direction is paramount. Besides strictly percentage returns, almost every player has one side that is weaker—the forehand or backhand—and you've got to be able to exploit that weakness.

Also, don't forget to go down the middle. First of all, it's the lowest part of the net and therefore easier to get the ball over. Plus you eliminate the opponent's angles. It's best to return down the middle against somebody like Pat Cash because he can hit such accurate angle volleys.

3. *Depth.* Actually, on return of serve this really means clearance of the net; in other words, how high your shot is when it clears the net. And that should be determined by what your opponent is doing. If your opponent is serving and volleying, your goal is to keep it low so his racquet appears below the white band when he contacts the ball. If he stays back, clear the net by at least three feet because your goal is to make the opponent play your return from deep in the court or, if possible, from behind the baseline.

Before you go out on the court for your match, you have to know what your opponent is likely to do. Against a serve-and-volleyer your prematch hitting should be geared to warming up that low return. If you can't practice for your opponent ahead of time, then spend the first couple of games getting the groove.

The best way to defeat a serve-and-volleyer is to return well. That means you have to know what a good return is. Blasting the ball for a winner is not the way to return. Your chances of getting it in are extremely low. Oh, you can go for it occasionally —if you pick the right occasion. But the most important return goes in almost all the time and neutralizes the volleyer. That means a low ball at the opponent's feet that makes him volley up. So you then have an easier ball to hit on the next shot.

Then there's the serve-and-volleyer who doesn't take a check step, who simply hits the serve and races to the net. The only answer is to lob. If the player is eliminating the check step and you don't lob, you're playing low-percentage tennis. He is rapidly decreasing the angle as he races to the net so only a great shot can beat him. Besides that, all his momentum is going forward. If you lob it's very tough for him to stop, backpedal, and hit an overhead.

4. *Spin*. I still feel too many players don't know how to hit a controlled return. The most important return on the backhand side is a chip to the backhand. I'm amazed how often Becker takes a high kicking serve to his backhand and tries to hit a topspin return. It makes no sense. But with the advent of the heavy topspin game, players think they have to hit the big shot every time. The low backspin shot that neutralizes a net-rushing server has almost been forgotten.

Also, on a wide, left-hander's serve to the ad court, it's a very poor percentage shot to hit a topspin backhand. It's very difficult to hit a crosscourt shot with topspin from there, so you'll tend to hit it right at them or down the line to their backhand volley, which they can easily put away to the open court.

5. *Speed*. It *is* important to learn to return the ball hard. It's another weapon, another variable your opponent will have to adjust to. For many players, however, it's the least difficult return to handle. They love a hard-hit ball hit right at them. If you dink them, throw a lot of spins and speeds at them, and really move them around, it gives them terrible trouble. Then, when you've got them dizzy, your big return can do some big damage.

One more tip for the return of serve: wait for the return of serve with a forehand grip. If you don't have time to change to a topspin backhand grip, the forehand grip still allows you to hit a solid backspin backhand return. Using a backhand grip

to hit a forehand return is an awkward and difficult task, and
it takes away your potential for a real weapon on the forehand.

THREE-MAN DRILL FOR THE RETURN OF SERVE

The best drill for the return of serve is to have two players
serving and volleying alternately to the returner. Play the point
out and then have the other player serve. This eliminates the
number-one problem when practicing the return of serve against
a serve-and-volleyer—boredom. With two servers bombing away
at a returner, he's always busy and the servers don't overwork
their arms.

THE CHIP-AND-CHARGE RETURN

If somebody is serving the ball short on their second serve,
make sure you get into the habit of attacking it. A great tactic
is to hit it into the corner deep, come in, and dare the guy to
pass you. That puts an enormous amount of pressure on the
server.

You can't "chip and charge," however, until you learn contact. That's the fundamental of the chip-and-charge return. A
player who takes a big backswing will never be able to chip and
charge. In fact, he'll never be able to return well at all. Thinking
"racquet back, follow through" will kill you on return of serve.

The time to use the chip-and-charge return is when the opponent is not passing well or when he hits a lot of first serves
into the net. You'll begin to see his second serve coming shorter
and shorter. That's the time to pounce.

The way to chip is to take the ball early like a volley. You
allow the momentum of your body to do the work with a minimum of racquet movement. Don't go for winners. The chip and
charge is a set-up shot. The idea is to try to get it as deep as
possible (generally to the backhand corner) with underspin.

Another important point is not to chip and charge unless
you can get to the IVP. That's where most players make their
mistake. A good chip-and-charger restrains from hitting the ball
hard to enable himself to get into the proper position. It doesn't
do you any good to blast the ball if it lets your opponent catch
you out of position. If you hit the ball hard and come in, you're
likely to make it only as far as the DVP (around the service line)
for your volley; from there you'll be a sitting duck for your
opponent's passing shots. The best chip-and-chargers are the
ones who hit the ball softly at the other player's feet. It forces

him to play a low-bouncing ball with nothing on it and hit it up in order to clear the net. At the same time they must try to generate enough pace on the ball to pass you—a very tough shot.

It's a lot easier to chip and charge from the deuce court because you can approach down the line to your opponent's backhand and you don't have far to go to get in proper position. From the ad court you have to take at least three or four extra steps to get into position if you are going to hit to your opponent's backhand (assuming he's right-handed). You can hit the ball down the line to his forehand from the ad court, but then that's probably chipping right into his power. And that is dangerous.

One final warning: if your opponent is hitting a great second serve—*do not come in*. All you'll end up doing is watching a lot of balls go flying by you for winners.

RUNNING AROUND YOUR BACKHAND RETURN

This is an important shot to have in your arsenal. I would encourage every player to practice it. The time to run around your backhand and crack your forehand is only on second serves, however. Do it when you get a slow-bouncing ball down the center or a little off center to the backhand side.

You must be sure that your opponent is serving and staying back, however. If you guessed wrong and he comes in, go for a winner, especially from the ad court. If you're receiving in the deuce court, you will end up in the middle of the court after you hit the shot, so it's not as critical to hit a winner. But you'd better hit a forcing shot at his feet or the point is over.

As soon as the server looks up at his toss to hit the ball, move to your left. You *must* be all the way over to the backhand side waiting with your forehand by the time the opponent hits the ball. On a normal-speed serve it's impossible to get all the way over in time if you wait until the server has actually hit the ball.

Running around your backhand is also extremely effective on a baseline rally. Graf and Lendl are masters of this shot. The best idea is to run to your left and hit the forehand back diagonally to the opponent's backhand. That's known as the inside-out forehand. You don't want to go down the line unless you can hit a winner. But it's a tough shot because the ball's coming into you and you're hitting over the high part of the net. Most important, you will put yourself way out of position when you hit down the line. You will be standing nearly in the ad court doubles alley, and you must run eight to ten steps to the other side of the court to get in position. And that is just about impossible to do. If you go crosscourt, however, you only have to take two or three short steps to get back in position.

CHAPTER 21

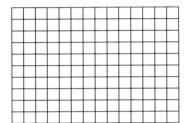

D–N–O:
THE YARDSTICK FOR TIME,
PLACE, AND CIRCUMSTANCE

THE D–N–O THEORY

A good golfer is usually hitting from a nice comfortable position in the middle of the fairway, while a beginner is usually in a trap or behind a tree. He's always out of position, and he's constantly forced to make difficult shots. But where the beginner really runs into trouble is when he tries to reach the green through the trees. It's a career shot even for a pro, and the hacker wonders why it took him six shots to get out of the woods. A beginning tennis player is also usually out of position, so he, too, is usually hitting a difficult shot. But instead of trying to hit safe shots, the beginning tennis player, like the beginning golfer, usually tries a shot even McEnroe would be overjoyed to make.

This may sound a bit odd, but most players don't even know when they're in trouble, and that leads us to an explanation of the defense–neutral–offense, or D–N–O, theory.

The D–N–O theory is based on two factors: the ball in relationship to the white band that runs along the top of the net and the position of both players on the court.

The white band is really the divisional part of the defensive-offensive theory of playing. When you contact the ball below the white band, you're in a defensive position. If you contact the ball above the white band, you're in an offensive position. Most players, therefore, make errors because they try to make an offensive shot when the ball is below the white band.

Concerning the second factor, the position of both players on the court, remember this:

1. If both players are at the baseline, the situation is neutral.

2. If both players are at the net, it's a neutral situation.
3. *But* if one player is at the net and one is at the baseline, you have an offensive-defensive situation.

For example, if one player is at the net (O) and he contacts the ball below the white band (D), he's neutralized (N). By the same token if a player at the net (O) gets the ball above the white band, he's in a double-offensive position and the point will probably end on that shot.

Remember it's not the D–O–N theory; it's the D–N–O theory. Don't try to go from defensive to offensive on one shot. The key word is *neutralize*. If you're in a defensive position with the other player at the net, you have two ways to neutralize your

D–N–O Theory: when your opponent is at the net *and* hitting a ball that is above the white band, he is in a double-offensive position.

183

If your opponent gets closer than the IVP (halfway between the net and the service line) the rule is to lob 100 percent of the time. Do not attempt to hit a passing shot.

opponent—you can either lob or make him volley from below the white band.

To do the latter, hit a low chip or a quickly dipping topspin shot. This forces the opponent to hit a volley with an arc to it, which is not an offensive volley, and thus you've neutralized him. But most players think the only effective shot is to hit the ball past the net man. And considering the fact that tennis players even at the top levels are able to hit outright winners on only 5 to 10 percent of their passing shots, that's not smart tennis.

Now, in terms of the D–N–O theory, if you want to neutralize an opponent who's serving and volleying, make him hit the first volley from below the white band. When I return serve I watch to see if my opponent contacts the ball below the white band, and if so I move in a little closer, knowing I'll probably have a chance for more of a setup or an offensive shot. If I hit a high shot to an opponent who's at the net, I have to be ready to react quickly because he has the potential to hit an offensive shot.

ADVANCED D–N–O

PLAYING THE NET

Most club players don't really understand why they should come to the net. They'll say to me, "I really don't know why I bother to go to the net. I hate it up there!" Because a player doesn't understand why he comes to the net, he has a fear of it and hence a lack of confidence.

The reason you come to the net to volley is to win the point. It may take a few volleys, but that's your goal up there, not to outsteady your opponent. You are on the offensive. The player who gets to the net first usually will win just because the pressure is on his opponent. The only exception is if your opponent has great passing shots, and even then, if you're serving and volleying well, your opponent won't get a decent opportunity to try a passing shot.

PASSING SHOTS

I studied the match charts at the 1987 United States Open, and in most three-set matches the average number of successful passing shots was three to five per match. At the U.S. Open! So, if you think about all the energy and importance placed on the passing shot, you have to wonder, is it worth it? Think how many attempts led to those three to five winners. It works out to about a 5 percent success rate. That's the most important thing to understand about passing shots—they don't work very often.

Most of the time a winner occurs without a player really knowing it's going to happen. I seldom say to myself when I set up to hit a passing shot: "I'm going to hit a winner!" I only have the potential to hit a winner because my opponent may simply outguess me. I may hit it perfectly down the line, but if he's standing there waiting, I've had it.

Many times when a player hits a passing shot, he's surprised he did it. And the better you get, the more surprised you are because you realize the difficulty of hitting an outright winner from the baseline against a well-positioned opponent. If your opponent has cut down your passing angles and has hit a decent volley or approach shot, your chances of hitting a passing shot are very slim.

Many times a player will attempt a passing shot and then watch where it goes, like Reggie Jackson watching a homer go out of the park. His opponent then reaches out and just taps it back over while he is still watching his "great" passing shot that wasn't a passing shot at all. He should have moved back into position and knocked off the next one. Don't assume the point has ended when you try a passing shot. If you hit it by your opponent, great. If not, you've got to be prepared.

The most important thing to understand when hitting a passing shot is that you should not be trying to hit the ball deep. As long as it gets past your opponent, you've hit a passing shot. In fact, a really good passing shot often lands short of the service line. That's why topspin is so valuable when passing. Even if the ball doesn't get past your opponent, it will probably put pressure on him. If he does get to it, he'll still have to make a great volley because the ball is probably at his feet.

One important question is whether to pass down the line or crosscourt. That is determined by several factors, including the position of your opponent at the net, your position, and your opponent's strengths—particularly whether he has a stronger backhand or forehand volley.

If your opponent has hit the ball into either corner and comes in and straddles the center service line, he's out of position. Always go down the line. If he's in proper position at the IVP, standing to the same side of the center service line as the side to which he hit the ball, then attack his weaker volley, forehand or backhand.

One other point: to hit an effective crosscourt passing shot, you've generally got to take a little pace off the ball because you've got a shorter area to hit into than down the line. You either have to hit the ball with more spin or hit it softer to make it land short. Most players don't pass well crosscourt because they try to hit the ball hard to the deep corner. If they hit the ball hard and far enough crosscourt to avoid a properly positioned net man, the ball will go out. That's physics.

SETUP TENNIS

You have to be able to identify when there's an opportunity for a winner and when it's time to play setup tennis. The percentage players actually hit more winners than the gamblers because their setup shots are giving them easier opportunities to hit winners. Lendl now hits many more winners than early in his career, when he simply blasted every ball. All because he sets up his passing shots and put-away volleys.

One of the main tools of setup tennis is the chip shot. A chip shot is a backspin shot with very little pace, one that just clears the net. A chip shot is hit exactly like a backspin drive except the racquet comes through a little slower and the follow-through is often shortened. One of the advantages of using backspin when the opponent is at the net is that backspin creates a slower ball. If you can make your opponent play a ball with little pace from below the white band, he'll have trouble doing anything with it.

A chip shot is useful because you can increase your variety and control with it. You can bust up someone's rhythm and hit very acute angles because the ball travels much more slowly, thus allowing you to ease it into the short corners of the court. Backspin is your control spin, and therefore you can do more with it in terms of control than you can with topspin. Use chip shots against players who need pace to volley well or against a player who changes grips at the net. The low chip is also effective against tall players because they often have trouble bending for low balls.

Remember, two things occur when you come to the net: (1) your opponent's errors automatically increase, and (2) he'll tend to hit the ball harder, which means his accuracy goes down. And accuracy is everything on passing shots. Until a player learns that he doesn't have to hit hard to hit a successful passing shot (he can chip or use topspin to drop the ball at his opponent's feet), the volleyer has a distinct advantage.

GOING FROM N TO O

Once you neutralize your opponent, once you go from D to N, you can't be complacent. Your goal must then be to get as quickly as possible from N to O. Or, before you know it, you'll find yourself back at D again.

It's the next shot after you've neutralized your opponent that is your opportunity to go on the offensive. The momentum has swung your way. That last shot has taken you to the neutral position and, as quickly as you can, you must try to figure out how to hit an offensive shot.

Club players especially are very casual about that next shot. They'll hit a good return to really put their opponent in trouble. Then the opponent will pop up a weak, short shot that barely clears the net—exactly the shot the player wanted—and it drops in for a winner because he was not ready to attack. He didn't take advantage of his setup shot.

Another common mistake is the reluctance to do anything

positive from the baseline. The opponent floats the ball back, and instead of saying, "OK, this is it. I'm through with N and I'm going on to O," the player will just push back another shot.

CONTACTING GROUND STROKES ABOVE THE WHITE BAND

If you contact a ball above the white band when you're at the IVP for the volley, your target should be one of the side T's so you can put the shot away. But if you're at the baseline, your goal is to put pressure on your opponent by putting pace on the ball. If you get a high bouncer near the baseline, do something with it, don't just get it back. You have a potential offensive shot because you don't need much of an arc to get it over the net. So, you can hit it flatter and harder and keep it in. Also, the ball will be in the air less time, which means your opponent has less time to get to it.

POINT COMBINATIONS

A point combination is the combining together of two or more shots in such a way that one shot makes the following shot more effective. The longer the point combination, however, the more chance you've got of flubbing it up. Either you or your opponent will miss before you even get a chance to pull it off. The ideal point combination therefore is two shots, but if you need it a three-point combination is all right.

Point combinations are very important to good strategy, but they must be learned through experience. They depend so much on the opponent, the circumstances, and your ability to execute specific shots that I could diagram literally hundreds of possibilities and still not give you any greater understanding of the game. So I'll simply introduce to you a couple of the most commonly used and least complicated combinations and let you build from there.

The use of the side T's to open up the court and produce greater angles is, perhaps, the most common method for putting together an effective combination of shots. Once the court is open there are many places your next shot can be hit to good effect.

One of the goals is to get your opponent outside the singles sidelines. Whenever you force your opponent outside the sidelines to get to a ball, you're in control of the point. He has a better angle from which to hit a shot, but his position leaves him vulnerable for almost any shot you hit back. He really only has two options. Either he goes for the outright winner down the line, or he can hook you back crosscourt to the opposite side T. The first is a low-percentage shot; the second leaves him extremely vulnerable to your down-the-line return.

Manuel Santana, the great clay-court player of the 1960s who won nearly every tournament of significance, including Wimbledon and the United States Championship, was perhaps the greatest practitioner of the "double side-T." He would hit the ball with tremendous topspin from side T to side T. Before his opponent could get to the ball it would already be outside the doubles alley. So back and forth his opponent would go for fifteen to twenty shots until his legs got rubbery. Then Manuel would hit a dropshot to the opposite corner for a winner. It was his favorite maneuver, and with it he won many major tournaments.

Another classic point combination involves the "diagonal theory." There are only two diagonals on each side of the court—from the point where the net and one singles sideline meet to the point at the baseline and the far singles sideline. If you hit a dropshot to one corner of the net and the next shot to the far diagonal corner at the baseline, you will force the opponent to run the most amount of steps possible to get to the ball.

The purpose of the diagonal theory is not necessarily to win the point, but to wear out your opponent, especially if he's a good ground-stroker, because fatigue often brings on a lack of muscle coordination and inevitably destroys a player's rhythm.

My personal realization of how effective the diagonal theory can be came in 1969 when I was playing at the Parklands Club in Nairobi, Kenya, which is at a fairly high altitude. My opponent hit dropshots and lobs at me unmercifully for the first three games. I was so worn out and confused I thought to myself, Geez! I don't know if I'll last the entire set! I figured if he could do this to me—and I don't tire easily—think of all those other players who would really be susceptible. And that's when I learned to open up the court.

CHAPTER 22

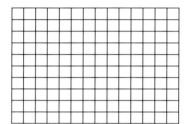

THE MIDCOURT GAME

PLAY THE RIGHT SHOT AT THE RIGHT TIME

If you look at the way the game is evolving right now, power ground strokes are very prominent and they will probably stay prominent for a long time to come. The speed of the game has increased at all levels, from the number-one player in the world to the B-level club player. Because of these strong shots, players are eliciting a lot of short returns from their opponents, balls landing at midcourt. So, on the next shot their feet are five or six feet inside the baseline, and they're setting up to hit a shot that they just don't know how to play.

First of all, few players ever practice that midcourt shot. They pound away at the baseline, then come to the net and hit there awhile. Very few pros ever teach it in a lesson either. But if you know how to play the midcourt game, you can dominate players at your level.

The midcourt is the most difficult position to play from. On a volley you're often taking the ball two or three feet behind the service line in the DVP. Or you're forced on a ground stroke to take a high floating ball with little pace on it. That's the one thing you can say for sure about a midcourt ball—it's usually got very little pace on it. If a ball is hit hard and it lands at midcourt, it'll keep you back. If it lands shorter than that it has to be hit softer. You just don't move into midcourt if the opponent has returned the ball fairly hard. So the essence of midcourt tennis is that you've got to deal with a ball with little pace.

You're in a position to hit a potentially offensive shot because first of all, you're moving into the net, and secondly, you're usually taking the ball above the white band. The problem is you don't have much to work with. It's like trying to hit a home run off a knuckleball. And a batter can be made to look very, very foolish swinging and missing at a good knuckler.

To play that midcourt shot, then, you've either got to crush that no-pace ball from there—a very difficult task to do consistently—or you have to understand how to really play the midcourt.

If you've got great confidence you treat the midcourt ball as a winner. But if you're like 99 percent of all players and you don't really believe you can bang that ball away consistently, you play setup tennis. The problem is most players, whether they have the ability or confidence, treat this shot as a putaway because it looks so darn easy.

Before we go any farther, let me clarify something. The midcourt is defined as the area from just a little inside the service line back to about four feet inside the baseline. This is not where the ball is but where your feet are. When I gave you the two rules of court positioning, I told you that you should never be caught at midcourt. And that still holds true. You should never *wait* there for your opponent's next shot. But when he's hit a short ball, you have to move into midcourt to hit the ball. But that's *after* your opponent has struck the ball, of course. Now it's your turn. But once you hit his short ball then you must once again get out of no-man's-land up to the IVP.

The whole point of the midcourt game is that it's the transition from the backcourt to the net. It's a one-shot ticket to the forecourt—a way to successfully approach the net. Never hit two balls in a row in the midcourt area. That's where club players get into a lot of trouble. They hit the ball and wait to see what their opponent is going to do, then they come in. But by then it's too late.

The pros often hit two balls in a row from midcourt too. But they're forced to do it because of poor shot selection. They often hit a ball so hard from there that they haven't got enough time to get to the IVP. And that's one of the most important considerations in playing the midcourt. You must hit your shot at a speed that allows you enough time to get in the proper position at the IVP for your next shot. This assumes you're planning to come to the net. On some midcourt shots you have the option of staying back.

Approaching from too deep in the court can get you in trouble as well. There are some areas where, no matter how slowly you hit the ball, you won't get to the IVP. And even if you could, the ball will be such a sitter you'd surely be in trouble anyway.

The mistake most players make is they hit the approach shot hard to put extra pressure on their opponent. The problem is if the shot comes back, *they're caught out of position.* Why hit the ball that hard if you're not going to hit a winner?

You actually go from an offensive position to defensive position by hitting the ball so hard. Players force themselves into making a midcourt volley because they've hit the wrong shot. Remember, the number-one rule in coming to the net is, if you can't get to the IVP for your first volley (other than on a first volley when serving and volleying), then do not approach the net because you will usually be out of position and easily passed.

Another bad error players make is they hit their approach crosscourt. Now, it's all right to hit the ball crosscourt and come in to the net, but you have to travel at least three or four steps farther to get in position at the IVP than if you had hit the ball down the line. According to the rules of court positioning that I explained earlier in the book, you must set up on the same side of the center service line as the ball when you're at the IVP. Of course, the down-the-line position at the IVP is closer than crosscourt. Therefore, you can hit the ball a little harder and approach from deeper in the court and still get in position at the net if you hit the ball down the line on approach shots.

If I hit a backhand approach to my right-handed opponent's backhand, I have to hit it a lot slower in order to get into position. Most players get a backhand and they think, I'm going to go back to my opponent's backhand. So they really pound it over there and they are not only out of position for a shot down the line from their opponent, but their momentum is carrying them away from a crosscourt return as well. So they're vulnerable to either side.

Probably the cardinal sin most club players commit when approaching is they hit their forehand approach crosscourt. Not only do they put themselves out of position, but they are hitting to what is most likely their opponent's most potent weapon— his forehand. And they wonder why they get passed so easily.

A player passes well almost invariably because of the way his opponent plays the midcourt game. Most players get passed because they're out of position, not because their opponent has great passing shots.

So you have to choose your approach wisely, especially against a good passer. You may take a ball deep in the court and hit the ball softly so you can get to the IVP, but that will give your opponent so much time he'll rifle a passing shot by you. If you hit the ball hard from deep in the court and try to get in, that's even worse because if you don't make it to the IVP, the court is completely open for even a mediocre passing shot.

So you've got to be patient against a good passer. Wait for the ball that's short enough so you can hit a penetrating shot and still get to the IVP.

When attempting an approach shot it's important to make sure that your feet are well inside the baseline, because it is essential that you take your next shot from the ideal volley position. Many players make contact with the ball too deep in the court and are forced to take their first volley somewhere around the service line, from which they can be easily passed.

THE TRAFFIC-LIGHT THEORY

So how do you decide when to come in and when to stay back? Well, fortunately, there's a handy guide to help you. It's called the traffic-light theory, and if you follow it carefully it's foolproof.

First of all you must understand something very clearly. It is the position of your feet on the court that determines whether you approach or stay back, *not* the position of the ball. A ball with heavy topspin that lands at the service line may actually force you behind the baseline, from which only a fool would try to come in.

The traffic-light theory divides the court up into three basic zones:

The red zone is behind the baseline. You should never run a red light and you should never approach from behind the baseline.

The traffic-light theory is a foolproof method of determining when to approach the net.

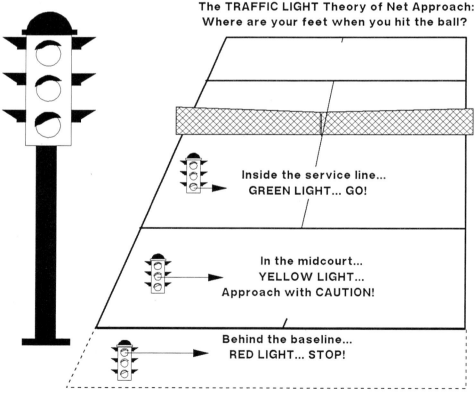

**The TRAFFIC LIGHT Theory of Net Approach:
Where are your feet when you hit the ball?**

Inside the service line...
GREEN LIGHT... GO!

In the midcourt...
**YELLOW LIGHT...
Approach with CAUTION!**

Behind the baseline...
RED LIGHT... STOP!

The green zone is the area from the service line up to the net. Once you're in this area, you *never* retreat. You always proceed to the IVP.

The yellow zone is the area from the baseline to the service line—no-man's-land. The yellow zone is itself divided into three zones. Pay close attention because these are the three most important areas when deciding whether to approach.

1. If you're in the forward third of the yellow zone, you go in most of the time. The only exceptions are if you are completely uncomfortable at the net or if the guy is really pounding his passing shots—and making them.

2. If you're in the back third of the yellow zone closest to the baseline, don't approach unless you're extremely confident, because it is a huge gamble to approach from that deep in the court. But there are those days when you just want to get to the net. Or maybe you're playing an opponent who just can't pass you. You can come in from almost anywhere on a guy who chokes whenever his opponent is at the net. If an opponent can't pass, get in because it's not a gamble. Normally, it would be poor-percentage tennis to come to the net on such a deep shot, but for this match and against this player, your percentages are to come in.

3. The middle third of the yellow zone is the area from which most approach shots are hit. Whether or not you approach from this area is determined by two factors. First, what is your mood that day? Are you confident? How is the match going? Some days you drive through every yellow light you see because you're in an aggressive mood. There are other days when you're out for a little drive, the kids are in the back, and you don't want to risk anything. The same thing happens in matches. You're comfortable at the baseline, so there's no need to come in.

The second factor when deciding whether to approach in this area is how well the opponent is passing.

APPROACHING DOWN THE MIDDLE

A seldom-used but often very effective strategy of the midcourt game is to approach down the middle, which cuts down the opponent's passing angles and makes it more difficult to hit a passing shot. Also a player will seldom step forward into a ball hit right at him! Normally, he'll take a step back to get out of the way. This forces the player back, with his momentum falling away from the ball. So he will probably not be able to counter your approach with a decent passing shot—and that's the whole purpose of a well-played approach. Instead, the opponent will probably try to hit a lob or chip you. Or he will try to hit a ball hard right at you because you've put him in a position in which there are virtually no angles to work with. This approach is particularly effective against power hitters.

THE BACKSPIN APPROACH

Most players at midcourt are physically and mentally out of control. And most of that is due to a deficiency in their technique. They don't have the physical tools to hit a controlled shot. If you don't have a backspin forehand and backhand, you don't have the equipment to handle the midcourt game. You must also have backspin ground strokes because backspin is your control spin. A topspin-only player can almost never have a good midcourt game.

The most important aspect of backspin when approaching is that it keeps the ball low. A low approach shot forces the opponent to hit the ball up in order to clear the net, and unless he hits an absolutely terrific topspin backhand, the ball will be coming up to you at the net for an easy putaway. The ball has to go up over the net, then back down in a very, very small area.

An infrequently used shot that is an important ingredient in the midcourt game is the backspin forehand. It is a very important shot and not just to approach with. The backspin forehand enables you to take charge of situations. You can't consistently hit a good lob if you can only hit a topspin forehand. If you want to dropshot effectively off that side, you've got to be able to hit backspin so you can jerk your opponent around.

THE APPROACH VOLLEY

Besides the first volley, when serving and volleying, there is another time when it's all right to hit a planned volley when you're not in the IVP. It's called an approach volley. But it should be reserved for very specific, well-thought-out situations. If your opponent is floating a lot of balls to you in the backcourt, it's smart to take that ball in the air at midcourt and volley it deep into a corner and get in to the IVP. Or if your opponent can't pass well but he's just staying back throwing up a lot of nothing balls, you can take the ball in the air, hit a volley to the corner, and make him pass you.

But remember, you should not try to hit a winning volley from there unless you're making everything that day. To hit an outright winner off that midcourt floater you've got to go for a side T, which is a tough shot from the DVP. Of course, if you're at the IVP or right on top of the net, then go ahead and get rid of it—just bang it away.

There are some players like Graf and Connors who take that ball in the air around the service line and hit a topspin volley winner. Now a topspin volley is a very difficult shot under any circumstance. But if you're superconfident and as good as Jimbo and Steffi, there's nothing wrong with that shot. Go for it!

But watch out for false confidence. If you don't hit that ball in almost *every* time, don't try it. You'll just be giving games away.

CHAPTER 23

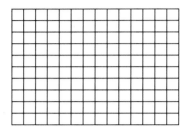

THE BIG POINTS

BIG-POINT MENTALITY

Tennis has a natural up-and-down flow to it, both physically and mentally. That's why the momentum of a match is constantly changing. Human concentration cannot be maintained on a steady, intense level all the time. Intensity is emotional and emotions go up and down. You can play three or four games going all out perhaps, but you'll be through for the match if you try. Therefore, you have to play hard and then push yourself into overdrive when you really need it.

What you must understand about tennis is that even if you win 6–1, you will often lose at least 40 percent of the points. In fact, players sometimes win matches in which they don't win a majority of the points played. They do, however, win the big points. Therefore, identification and awareness of the big points is mandatory if you are to be a good player. The big points are weighted so heavily compared to the rest of the points that if you don't concentrate on them, you simply don't understand the nature of the game.

The good player doesn't just go out there and play one point at a time. That implies that all the points are of equal importance. That's like saying all the chess pieces are of equal value, that you'd trade a king for a pawn. There are a lot of big points in every tennis match and a few very big points, and the player who focuses his attention, his energy, and his concentration on those points will almost always win the match.

The biggest point, of course, is match point. If you never win a match point, you will never win a match. But there are other big points in a match, and it is crucial to the outcome of a match that you know what points are big points and that you are always particularly aware when you're playing one.

The third and fifth points of every game are the most important points in tennis. If you win both the third and fifth points of every game, you will win approximately 80 percent of your games. That's fact based on statistics we've done of match play at all levels.

There is an overwhelming psychological and strategical advantage to being ahead 40–0 rather than 30–15, and that's the difference between winning or losing the third point. The fifth point is even more crucial. A 30–30 game can go to a game point for you at 40–30 or break point against you at 30–40. That, in a nutshell, is all the difference in the world.

Because you can end the game on it, 40–30 is also a big point. I recommend serving and volleying at 40–30 regardless of the surface. Put the pressure in your opponent's corner and see how he handles it. At 40–15 an opponent may gamble, but very few players gamble on the return of serve at 40–30. Who wants to just throw the game away? The first principle of good returning is to make the server hit a first volley, make him work for the point.

The fifth and seventh games are the most important games to win. The psychological aspects of tennis are so significant that the edge gained by winning one important game can make a runaway of a close set. A close set at 4–2 becomes a runaway at 5–2 or a tooth-and-nail battle at 4–3. Other examples: 3–1 becomes 4–1 or 3–2; 4–0 becomes 4–1 or 5–0; 3–3 becomes 4–3 or 3–4. Those are very crucial splits.

You've probably already figured out that there are also "superbig points"—times when big points and big games coincide. On the fifth point of the seventh game, a circuit pro will run out of his shoes trying to win the point. Yet the club player who is totally unaware of the significance of the point may decide to try for a big backhand that hasn't much chance of going in.

HOW TO PLAY THE BIG POINTS

The difference between the champion and the average player is that the champion is not tentative on the big points. He takes it to his opponent. Controlled aggression is the key. Force your opponent, but do it within the confines of percentage tennis and your match priorities.

Your frame of mind on big points should be calm, conservative, collected, and confident. If a big point is at hand, that's when you have to be the most composed. Pumping your fists and slapping your thighs very rarely does anything but cause bruises. Usually the champions take a little bit longer to get their body relaxed, get their thoughts collected, get their breathing back to normal. And then they play the point with a clear mind.

Also, play the percentages. Don't gamble. Don't try to come up with a big shot to win the big points. You'll often see players at all levels try to hit an ace on match point. What does a champion do? He gets the first serve in, comes to the net, hits a good volley, and makes the opponent pass him.

Put the pressure on your opponent on big points. It's a very rare human being who, when you put him under pressure, can counterpressure you. Particularly, watch a player's strokes at key points. That's when you can most easily spot his weaknesses, because that's when he's most nervous and therefore most vulnerable to a breakdown. If he has a shaky forehand, it will do most of its shaking on the big points.

Instead of pressuring their opponent, however, many players put the pressure on themselves by trying to do something that is over their heads. You don't raise your game for the big points by trying to hit impossible shots. You do it by playing percentage tennis very, very well. Three of the best big-point players in the modern game have been Billie Jean King, Rod Laver, and Mats Wilander.

PART IV
MIND GAMES

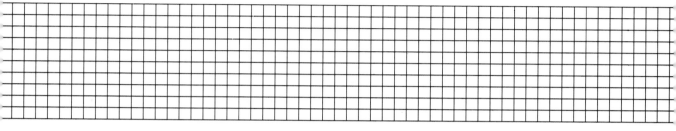

CHAPTER 24

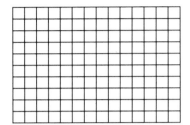

COMMITMENT AND COURAGE

JUST ONE MORE SERVE

Leonard Bergelin, Björn Borg's coach, ran the Swedish Junior Team. And every day at the end of practice he'd call all the kids in to take a shower. And, of course, they all came running, eager to get in after a tough day of workouts. Everyone except Borg. Bergelin would have to go out three or four times and yell at Björn to come on in. Borg would be out there with a bucket of balls hitting serves. And he'd yell back at Bergelin, "Just one more serve! Just one more serve!"

That became the running joke about Borg. "Just one more serve!"

Ivan Lendl's rise to the top was no accident either. He was willing to do whatever it took to become and stay number one. Whether it was going out and finding a good coach or going through hours of grueling physical training or building a tennis court in his backyard to match the surface at the U.S. Open, he did it all.

To succeed in tennis, or anything for that matter, you must have a commitment—a commitment to practice, to understand the game, and to change your game if necessary. Many times a player is looking for a quick cure when he comes to a pro, and instead he gets a quick shuffle. Often he's getting what he deserves. It takes a firm commitment to improve—not just a once-a-week lesson and lots of complaining in between. Often a student will come to me for a lesson, then return seven days later and be frustrated in his next lesson. So I'll ask, "How much did you practice?" and he'll reply, "Well, I haven't had a chance."

Commitment can enable you to defeat the limitations of your

body, to go beyond what is considered your potential. Most players have the illusion, however, that if you simply practice long enough you will reach that potential. But practice can actually make your game decline. There are only two things you can practice: bad habits and good habits. Many people regress in life because they practice bad habits, and that pattern is transferred to the tennis court.

It's the quality of your practice and the quality of your understanding that determine if you will improve. And maintaining a high quality for a sustained period of time is most important. One day of practice every other month will not help because, among other things, what you practice today often won't show up in your game for several months. So you've got to keep at it.

The typical club player won't practice if the day isn't perfect. If it's too windy or too hot or he doesn't feel that well, he doesn't even consider practicing. You'll often hear him say something like, "My game gets worse when I practice in the wind," which means when the day isn't just perfect he can't play a match because he's never practiced in those conditions.

For most players practice is a waste of time because they go out there without a purpose. Without a sense of purpose there is no meaning to your practice. In other words, when you step out on the court, for a big match or just for another practice, you must have a plan. A plan, a sense of purpose, heightens your awareness of what you can or cannot do. And if you can't do it in practice, there's little hope of doing it in a match. So, when setting up drills for practice, simulate what might happen in a game. Go for the target zones, never let a ball bounce twice, run your partner around, and chase down everything he hits.

THE FIGHTING SPIRIT

If I could name one ingredient in a player's game that means the most to success, it would be the desire to fight, to never give up. Most players don't know how to transcend the physical and mental problems that bombard them. What distinguishes all great athletes is that they can draw upon a reserve. In the last few games of a five-set match there isn't a lot of classic form or strategy—it's mostly desire. When your strokes have fallen apart and your body is cramped or starting to cramp and your main desire is just to sit down or get a drink of water, you've got to rely on guts.

You have to learn how to fight. First of all, the fighting spirit should be instilled young. It's tough to instill it in an adult who's already fitted for a lazy chair. Oh, I've seen it happen. But that player has to motivate himself to become a fighter. Maybe you say it's just not that important for you to go all out on the tennis court. And that's fine. But if you spend hours and hours and years and years of your life on the tennis court trying to improve, then it probably *is* worth it.

Having guts is partly experience. You can develop a gutsy attitude. Those who go the distance learn to deal with the different stresses involved in winning, including such things as fatigue. I learned, for example, a breathing technique to use after a long, grueling point. Instead of the normal reaction of taking huge gulping breaths of air (which causes hyperventilation), I would exhale several quick short breaths without inhaling any air. This reduces the level of carbon dioxide in your system (which causes shortness of breath), and you're then able to recover from oxygen deprivation four or five times more quickly.

Also, you've got to learn to fight your way through adversity. Anybody can play well when things are going his way, when the conditions are to his liking and the opponent never makes him feel uncomfortable. But if you never push yourself, if you refuse to do anything that doesn't feel comfortable, how will you ever know your limits? Remember, you should always have a game strategy and back-up strategies, but when those fail, the final strategy is guts.

LEARNING TO WIN

Many times you see two players on the court and the player with the worse-looking strokes, who can't hit the ball nearly as well as his opponent, wins the match. Which shows that a player can hit the ball well and yet not know how to win.

To win tennis matches it's important to understand the nature of the game. The fact is, most tennis matches are lost not won. The good tennis player doesn't blast his opponent off the court. He forces his opponent to lose games, to make errors, to lose his concentration, especially during crucial points.

Most players love to hit the big shot to win a point. But the successful big shot is so infrequent that it's given way too much weight. There are many more ways to beat a player than by blowing him off the court. But the crowd loves a big winner and so do most players. If you try to blow a guy off the court, more often than not you just end up blowing a bunch of shots.

LEARNING FROM A LOSS

Go to any tournament and ask a player who just won what he learned from the match, and he'll give you about a thirty-second answer. Then ask the player who just lost and you'll get tennis's version of the filibuster. We human beings, regrettably, seem to learn only from our losses. Winning is such a big deal in our lives that we forget how we won. One of the most difficult things in life is to ride the crest of the wave and still maintain perspective. When you lose a match, however, it's usually because you were challenged. You were called upon to do things you couldn't do. So, you find out what's wrong with your game when you lose.

Often the most valuable experience in a loss is finding out there's someone better than you. So frequently I'll see players who have enormous egos about their games—for no logical reason. They're number one where they play and they think Lendl is in trouble. Or how about the top guy at the club who's never entered an outside tournament (because he knows he'd get annihilated), but the size of his ego would rival the Goodyear blimp. These players find the level at which they can dominate and never venture out of it because they don't want to go through the ego problem of losing. They never challenge themselves.

MOMENTUM—THE STRUGGLE FOR CONTROL

Tennis is a game of momentum. It's a battle of two players, one getting the best of the other, then the other player coming back. There is always a struggle going on out on the tennis court, a tug of war in which one player or the other has the momentum, the upper hand. And that player fights to maintain his dominance. But the momentum shifts back and forth from player to player. You can constantly see the game seesawing.

You have to remember, even though the match is rolling along in your favor, that the other guy can pick up his game at any time and if you don't pick up your game, he'll take over the match.

You'll start to wonder all of a sudden, What's wrong with my game? Well, nothing's wrong with it. The other guy just raised the level of play. That's why you've got to forget your own game. Put your focus on the other court. What's the other guy doing? Why is he suddenly controlling me? What has he done differently?

THE MOOD OF THE MATCH

Tennis is played by human beings, so our humanness is an essential ingredient in the game of tennis. The moods that go on during a match are varied and numerous. If you could get inside a player's head and watch his mood swings throughout the match, it would be amazing. Players will go from sheer terror to the greatest euphoria within minutes. Almost from one shot to the next. A player, for example, will hit a lousy lob and think, Oh, what a horrible shot. But his opponent will mishit the overhead and when the guy runs it down and hits a winner, he starts pumping his fists in exaltation even though only a second before he was cussing himself for his lousy lob. It happens all the time.

These moods are human nature. They're a natural part of the game. It's *controlling* your moods that's important. Keep things in perspective. When you hit a great shot don't immediately let it go to your head and think you're a great player. Because then you'll start going for all the big shots even when the priorities and percentages are dead against it. How often do you see a player hit an ace and then double fault on the next point? That happens mostly because the player tries to hit another ace. Instead of realizing that a lot of hitting an ace is luck, he starts to think he can do it on every serve.

On the other hand, don't get down on yourself if you hit a bad shot or two or three. How many times have you heard a player mutter, "I can't hit a thing today"? How true is that statement? He misses a couple of backhands and he's convinced his whole game stinks. Then he'll hit a lucky shot and suddenly he's up again.

Tennis is an up-and-down roller coaster of a sport. The momentum shifts constantly from game to game, from point to point. Sometimes it shifts during a point. So try your best to keep your emotions from going on that roller coaster ride. That's the best way to keep yourself and your game under control.

Play steady, think steady, and keep your moods steady. That's the way to play the most effective tennis. Avoid the temptation to go wild when you hit a winner or hang your head when you make an error. If you miss a shot, so what? Tennis is a game of misses. Expect to miss some and you won't be so disappointed when you do. If you believe that you should never miss, however, you're in for a lot of disappointment playing tennis.

Struggle against bad moods. If you get down on yourself, fight to bring your mood back to level again. And try to exploit your opponent's bad mood. Young players, for example, are prone to streakiness. If they hit a winner, they can suddenly lift their game for a stretch in which they can do *nothing* wrong. They hit everything in and they hit it hard. But one bad shot can ruin them for games at a time.

On the other hand, look at Lendl. You very rarely see a match like 6–1, 1–6, 6–2 from Lendl. Lendl doesn't have big ups and downs. He'll often lose a first set, but usually in a struggle. But once he gets on top of his opponent he steamrolls the guy. He's very good at breaking up an opponent's momentum and then not letting him get it back. Ivan struggles with a player and stays in there and when he finally gets on top of the guy he buries him. He takes the momentum and runs with it.

The higher up you move in tennis, the less you can gain the momentum in a match because at the higher levels the players understand that the mood of the match is all-important. If they lose the momentum, if they give up fighting even for a few points, they can lose control of the match forever. The smart players won't allow you to take control.

The way to maintain momentum is to just play your game and not to try to increase your momentum. The other player will do that by playing worse if you continue to apply pressure. If you try to increase your momentum, what you often end up doing is going for better and better shots. You've gotten over-confident. That is the chink in your armor that is just what the opponent needs to come back. You will start trying foolish, impossible shots, your opponent will get back his confidence, and suddenly you've got a match on your hands again.

At that point it's easy to start thinking your game is going down when actually all you did was try a couple of ridiculous shots. That's how you lose momentum. And the match.

CHAPTER 25

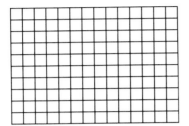

CONCENTRATION AND CONFIDENCE

CONCENTRATION

Concentration is a fundamental of the game. If a person can't concentrate, their capacity for learning anything is severely limited and they won't be able to play the tough points of a match. So concentration is critical for everyone from the beginner right on up the ladder to the touring pro.

Many players visit sports psychologists to increase their powers of concentration because it's so important. I'm not against sports psychologists; in fact, a good one can do wonders for your game. But I have seen players make tremendous leaps in their concentration simply by doing three things. First, they focus on their opponent that day using the fundamentals of investigating the other court. Second, they use big-point mentality; they know the big points and focus their concentration on them. And third, they play the points one at a time.

Putting your focus on the opponent, on the other court, takes your mind off yourself, your strokes, your worries, your aches and pains, and puts your mind instead squarely on tennis.

If you're out there worrying about your own game, you've got two things going on at once: trying to fix up your strokes and trying to play the match. You become your own opponent. Don't get hung up on your side of the court. Thinking about your own game and how you feel comes from fear and creates more fear. When things go wrong your mind begins to panic.

Instead, if you focus on your opponent, you can concentrate better because your mind will be busy with the game. It's fun to concentrate on your opponent. It becomes a challenge. Being able to read your opponent is exciting! And when you're having fun, fear remains in the far reaches of your mind, unable to harm you.

Big-point mentality is another important tool to keep your concentration up. You've got to *budget your concentration*; you can only be intense for so long. It's simply impossible to keep your intensity high for every point. The human mind doesn't work that way. So you've got to choose very carefully when to turn on your full concentration.

Finally, play each point one at a time. Don't visualize shaking hands and what's going to happen after you win or what people are going to say. Play the match point by point. A player who lets his mind get too far ahead of himself won't be able to concentrate on the job at hand.

CONFIDENCE

Complete confidence is a total lack of fear. Since fear is the greatest enemy of concentration on the court, probably the greatest asset a player could ever have is confidence. But confidence is a very fragile thing. It's got to be handled with care.

Everybody chokes and everybody has their moments of fear. But you can't let it take over. You can't give into it. You must realize that tennis is a game of choking. McEnroe chokes. Lendl chokes. Navratilova chokes. It's going to happen. It's normal. So get used to it. Don't fear those moments. Don't fear choking. It's part of the game.

The antidote to fear is a positive mental attitude. True champions refuse to be affected by the fear of losing. And it's the fear of losing that really paralyzes players, not losing itself. What will the other people think if I lose to this guy? What will happen to my ranking?

If you keep it all in perspective, the fear is easy to handle. A year from now there will be only a couple of people on this planet who will remember that match you lost.

BODY LANGUAGE

Borg once said he was so afraid to walk on the court some days that his whole body would be trembling. When he'd get to the fifth set he could hardly hold on to his racquet. But nobody ever knew that because Björn would never allow his emotions to show. When you played Borg you thought you were playing a man who knew no fear because he showed no signs of it.

The fact is if you walk and talk like a winner, you can often turn a match around. Look at Jimmy Connors. You can never tell the match score by his body language. Connors is always

Often you can tell who's winning a match simply by watching the players' body language. It is essential that you avoid negative body language such as dropping your head or your racquet or slouching your shoulders. Act as if you're winning the match no matter what the score. Walk tall and stride confidently.

bouncing up and down. He's usually the first one out of the chair at the changeover. He's ready to go. I've never seen Jimmy not fight for points, no matter what the score. And many times it has helped him win matches he looked hopelessly out of because if there's a letdown, any loss of confidence or concentration by his opponent, Connors is ready to pounce.

If you can control your emotions on the surface, you can control them underneath. That's the key. When you're trying not to let anyone know how you feel, you work extra hard not to let your emotions run wild. Never let your opponent know

you're afraid. Walk with confidence. Keep your head up. Don't blurt out statements like, "Boy, what a choke!" It may, in fact, be true that you're choking. But it's dumb to let your opponent know it. All that does is make his confidence soar.

André Agassi has great body language. If you look at Agassi you can't tell if he's winning or losing. He exudes confidence even when he's in trouble. That's what you want to shoot for. No matter what the score, try to give the impression that all is right with your game and the world. If you do, you can fool not only your opponent, but youself as well. Your good attitude will rub off on you and your game.

BUILDING CONFIDENCE

A strong foundation is your safety net. If you start to choke go back to the fundamentals. Go back to the basics of the stroke and get back to getting the ball over the net.

Also, if you're on a losing streak it's often a good idea to play in lesser tournaments or against lesser opponents and learn how to win again. Build up your confidence and the winning attitude. On the circuit I often played in local weekend tournaments (I was usually out of the pro tournament in the early rounds) where I knew I could get to the semis or the finals and probably win. Then I'd go back to the circuit and I'd be much sharper because I'd developed a winning attitude. Losing is so often just a frame of mind. You've got to break that frame of mind and learn the trick of winning.

PLAYING HAPPY

Have you ever watched a great tennis match and then been charged up to go out and play? Your first five or six games are often unbelievable because you're on a high—you're inspired. Can you imagine how you'd play if you could maintain that level of excitement for tennis all the time?

I've always admired Jimmy Connors. He's just bubbling with enthusiasm for the game of tennis. He had that same excitement for the game when he was a kid and he's carried it right onto center court. He is one of the few players in the modern era who truly loves playing tennis and competing.

If players could maintain enthusiasm they could improve rapidly. Often the guy who plays twice a week can improve faster than the guy who plays five times a week because he's more eager. You can improve faster by playing hard for one hour a day than going through the motions for six hours. Connors is one of the hardest practicers on the circuit, and yet often he'll only practice for forty-five minutes or so. But when he comes off the court he's dripping from head to toe with sweat and his practice partner is exhausted. As soon as you lose your enthusiasm during a practice session, it's better to just head for the showers.

Many players today have lost the attitude that tennis is fun to play. Play happy. Have a good attitude. Next time you're out there grumbling, snap yourself out of it. Play happy and you'll love the game, you'll love your enthusiasm, and you'll improve because of it. Just your own sheer enjoyment of the game can catapult you over the man who fights himself on every point.

SET THREE

OFF THE COURT

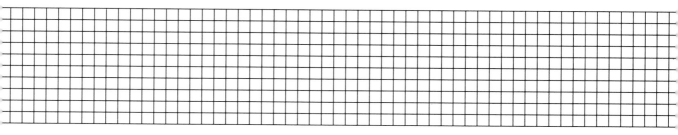

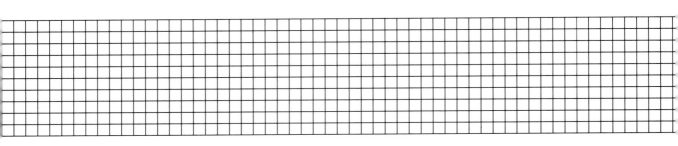

CHAPTER 26

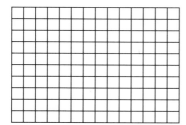

COMPETING PHYSICALLY

CONDITIONING IS A FUNDAMENTAL

Just as well-executed ground strokes are a fundamental of a good tennis game, so too is conditioning. Many players need basic lessons in health more than they need tennis lessons. The simple fact is that if your body is not in tune, it's hard to tune up your game. You've got to eat and sleep right and exercise your entire body regularly.

You sometimes hear a player say, "I was in the zone today. I could do no wrong. I really felt great." We've all had those days. Well, whether you realize it or not, those are often the days when you're feeling extra healthy. If you want to make a breakthrough in your tennis game, make a breakthrough in your health. If you're carrying thirty or forty extra pounds, or if your muscles are in poor condition from lack of exercise, you'll probably never be a good tennis player.

Conditioning becomes more and more important as you get better. You'll hear this all the time from neophyte players: "Oh, gee, I like racquetball better because I don't get any exercise playing tennis." But that's because they're not really playing the game. Tennis gets very physically demanding the better your game becomes.

Let's face it, if you're dragging around an extra thirty, forty, fifty pounds, you're at a disadvantage against a player who's in shape. Even if you can do all right in the first set, it's doubtful you could pull out a tough three-setter. You'll be playing at less than half your potential by the end of the match.

Physical fitness aids your mental game as well. If you feel good on the court, you are naturally going to feel confident that you can do the job at the end of a long, grueling match.

AEROBICS

The technical definition for a fit person is someone who has the ability to effectively take oxygen into their body and use it at the cellular level. In other words, you want to be able to get oxygen to the cells so they can do their job. That's why you need basic aerobic conditioning. Aerobic conditioning is the foundation of all physical fitness.

Even though tennis is not technically an aerobic sport, your heart rate still stays up there pretty high while playing, especially at the higher levels of the game. So a good aerobic program is a must for the serious tennis player.

You don't have to go to a gym for an aerobic workout. An aerobic program in your home or office or hotel room when traveling is easy to set up and maintain.

If you need help setting up your own program, pick up a copy of my book, *The Aerobic Workout Book for Men*. This book is great for women too! I emphasized "for Men" only in order to attract more men to the great benefits of aerobics. Readers may order my workout book by writing to:

Workout Book
PBI
2203 Timberloch Place, Suite 126
The Woodlands, TX 77380

Enclose ten dollars (about half the cover price including shipping) and I'll send the book to you.

CONDITIONING EXERCISES

One of the nice advantages of tennis is that it's a great sport for overall fitness. Playing a lot of tennis can eliminate the necessity for lots of detailed exercises. There are, however, certain areas of the body that need special attention for you to play better tennis.

After conversations with many doctors and fitness experts and years of personal experience with pros and students, I found there are three parts of the body that need particular strengthening for tennis—the wrists, the ankles, and the stomach muscles.

STRENGTHENING THE WRISTS

The tendons and muscles of the wrist must be strong because it's the wrist that connects the racquet to the rest of the body. And the wrist becomes particularly important in emergency situations and when executing many of the more advanced touch shots that take a firm but flexible wrist.

To strengthen the wrists, do "rope rolls." Tie one end of a rope about four feet long to the middle of a stick about eighteen inches long. Tie the other end of the rope to a one-pound weight. Then with one hand on either end of the stick, wind the weight up from the ground to the stick by rolling the rope around the stick. Then back down again. Repeat several times.

KEEPING THE ANKLES STRONG AND FLEXIBLE

The ankle is very injury prone because it is the joint closest to the ground and so it takes the most pounding. Most ankle injuries happen because the ankle is not strong and flexible at the same time. Usually, the tendon will snap because it has not been prestretched. So, special attention should be given to stretching the ankle.

STRENGTHENING THE STOMACH MUSCLES

Just about every movement in tennis, including the serve, the overhead, and the ground strokes, initiates from the stomach. The stomach is the hinge of the body. Since the belly button is the center of gravity, strength and control of the abdomen is key to almost every phase of the game. You'll be quicker off the mark with a smaller, tighter, more muscular stomach. The whipping motion of the arm on the serve actually starts at the stomach. And when you're in the air hitting an overhead, any power must come from the stomach.

Cross-body sit-ups are the best exercise for strengthening a "jelly belly." Lie on your back and bring your knees up until your feet are flat on the ground. Then alternately lift up and touch your right elbow to your left knee, back down, then touch the left elbow to your right knee. Start with about twenty repetitions and build up from there. Also, to protect your back, remember to keep the small of your back flat on the ground.

SHAPING UP THE LEGS

To get the legs in shape for tennis, I don't recommend jogging. There's nothing wrong with jogging; it's great exercise and also helps build your wind. But it is not the best sort of running for tennis. I recommend instead short sprints or my favorite "shuttle runs."

Place one racquet on the ground at the net with ten balls

on the strings and one racquet at the baseline. Then, starting at the baseline, transfer all ten balls, one at a time, to the racquet at the baseline. This start-and-stop-and-bend motion is identical to what your legs go through in a match.

Other excellent exercises for developing stamina and strength in the legs are skipping rope and playing lots of minitennis.

STRETCHING AND FLEXIBILITY

Flexibility is the range of possible movement in a joint or series of joints (as when the spinal column is involved). The need for flexibility varies from sport to sport. In tennis, because of the demands put on every part of the body, it is all-important. Even for the armchair athlete flexibility is important. An improper gait caused by stiffness results many times in lower-back problems, and maintaining flexibility prevents or relieves the aches and pains that grow common with age and often foreshadow arthritis.

Basically there are three reasons why we need to stretch our muscles:

1. To improve our range of motion
2. To help relieve muscle soreness after physical overexertion
3. To help prevent injury (as by loosening up your ankles before a match to prevent strains)

There are two types of stretching exercises: there's the dynamic or ballistic method, in which bobbing, bouncing, and jerky movements are used, and the static method, which involves holding a position for a set period of time while locking the joints involved into one spot that places the muscles and connective tissue at their greatest possible length.

Both methods satisfactorily stretch the muscles, but there are three distinct advantages to static stretching. First, there is less danger of overstretching muscle tissue. Remember that the muscles are like rubber bands. If you continue to pull on a rubber band in quick, jerky motions, it probably will break (like tearing a muscle), but if you gradually stretch the rubber band, you will eventually feel the limit of its elasticity. In static stretching, this is where you hold the position. Second, in static stretching you use less energy because there is less motion. Third, ballistic stretching often causes muscular soreness, whereas static stretching can actually relieve it.

The following stretching exercises can be done before you play tennis to help loosen up your muscles and avoid injury. You can expand these exercises for a more comprehensive stretching program designed to improve your overall flexibility.

1. Stretching the calf muscles. Stand, feet together, approximately one racquet's length away from the net post, with your hands resting on the post and your arms slightly bent. Keeping your heels on the ground and your legs straight, lower your hips toward the post. When you feel the stretch in your calves, hold the position for thirty seconds. Relax and repeat once.

2. Stretching the Achilles tendons. Starting from the same position with heels on the ground, bend your knees forward toward the net post. When you feel the stretch in your Achilles tendons, hold the position for thirty seconds. Relax and repeat once.

3. Stretching the quadriceps and ankles. Place your left hand on the net post for balance and bend your right leg up behind you. With your right hand, grasp your toes and pull up until you feel the stretch. Hold the position for thirty seconds. Do the same exercise on the left side. Repeat once for each leg.

4. Stretching the ankles. Using the net post for balance, raise your right foot off the ground slightly and slowly rotate the foot at the ankle in a circle for thirty seconds. Do the same with the left foot.

5. Stretching the buttocks. Standing upright, lift the right leg upward, bending it at the knee. Grasp just below the knee, using both hands with fingers interlocked, and pull the leg toward chest. Hold for two seconds, then switch legs. Repeat for each leg at least five times.

6. Stretching the hamstrings and lower back. Sit on a bench, left leg down beside you and right leg straight out on the bench in front of you. Keeping your right leg straight and your toes pointed forward, lean toward the foot with your arms extended. Touch the toe if possible, or whatever point you can reach without straining. Eventually your head may also touch your knee. Hold the position for thirty seconds. Repeat on other side. *Note*: Do not bounce or jerk down. Ease your way down.

7. Stretching the hamstrings, lower back, and calves. Starting from the same position on the bench, flex the foot with the toes pointing upward. Do the exercise as before. Eventually you will be able to hold onto the foot and pull the toes toward you. Repeat with the left leg.

8. Stretching the muscles on the side of the body. Stand with your feet apart, both arms above your head holding the racquet. Bend to the right until you feel the stretch along your side. Hold for five seconds and then bend to the left. Repeat three times on both sides.

9. Stretching the shoulders, upper arms, and back. Hold the racquet behind your back with both hands. Bend forward, keeping the arms and legs straight, and allow the arms to extend upward and forward (over your head, if possible.) Hold this position for ten seconds, relax, and repeat three times.

10. Stretching the shoulders, upper arms, and back. Holding the racquet in your right hand, allow it to hang down your back. Reach behind you and grasp the throat of the racquet with your left hand and pull the racquet down, pointing the right elbow to the sky. Hold this position for thirty seconds, then do the exercise with the left arm. Repeat once for both arms.

INJURY PREVENTION

Most injuries in tennis are related to improper warm-up or conditioning. Ankle sprains and knee injuries occur with the greatest frequency to players who haven't participated in any exercise in months and then jump right out on the court and try to go full blast. And a major cause of sore arms is the FBI. You know, "first ball in." A player won't take any warm-up serves; instead he tries to blast the first few serves at a hundred miles an hour and then wonders why his arm just fell off. Most injuries are caused by foolishness, not weakness. The majority of injuries can be avoided by proper conditioning and flexibility.

FIVE WAYS TO GET TENNIS ELBOW

There are five basic ways to get tennis elbow:

1. *Placing the thumb behind the grip for more support on backhands.* When you place your thumb behind the racquet handle on backhands, the tendency is to point the elbow out toward the ball and push at the ball from the elbow. This makes the elbow the center of rotation. But properly executed, the swing should start at the shoulder, not the elbow, because the shoulder is a rollable (ball-and-socket) joint capable of the rotation necessary to swing the arm. The elbow, however, is only a bendable joint, and the strain caused when a player swings from there is one of the chief causes of tennis elbow. In order

to prevent undue strain on the arm that may lead to injury, the thumb should be a nonfunctional digit on the backhand, wrapped around the grip with all the other fingers.

2. *Straightening the arm on a forehand.* I'm amazed that even today so many players are still hitting their forehands with a straight arm. Because of a lack of understanding of anatomy, they're setting themselves up for an arm injury. On contacting the ball, force is transferred from the wrist to the elbow. If the arm is bent, the biceps, the main stabilizing muscles of the arm, are working and the force is transferred along the biceps to the shoulder joint, which is capable of absorbing this shock. When the arm is straight, however, the biceps are relaxed (the triceps have taken over) and the force stops in the elbow region. This continual shock to the elbow joint will usually result in injury.

One of the most common ways of developing tennis elbow is to prepare and make contact with a perfectly straight arm on the forehand. When the arm is in this position the bicep is completely relaxed and all force is transferred instead to the elbow.

Another way to develop tennis elbow is to either pronate or supinate your arm when hitting the ball.

Still another way to develop tennis elbow is to contact the ball on your serve with a straight arm and a locked wrist.

3. *Serving with a straight arm and a firm wrist.* Once again, if the arm is straight the biceps have extended fully all the shock transfers from the wrist to the elbow. If you're having trouble snapping your wrist, loosen the last three fingers of the racquet hand completely and grip the racquet with only the thumb and forefinger. Since the last three fingers control the tendons that tighten the wrist, this will ensure a loose wrist.

4. *Whipping topspin.* One of the most common causes of tennis elbow is trying to put excessive topspin on the ball when hitting ground strokes by rolling over the top of the ball with the wrist and elbow. Again, this is asking the elbow to act as a rollable joint, which it cannot do without risk of injury.

223

5. *Bad timing.* The final basic way of getting tennis elbow is plain old bad timing. Mishitting the ball because of bad timing strains the muscles and joints the same way unexpectedly missing a stairstep can wrench you. The ball comes through faster or slower than you thought and the resulting mishit causes a tearing of muscle tissue.

This problem is much more prevalent among men than women. Men usually try to pound the ball long before they have the timing perfected. The best remedy is to simply stop swinging so hard. Slow down. Pretend your arm is moving in slow motion.

DIET AND YOUR TENNIS GAME

At the 1988 Intercollegiate Coaches Association Convention, I spoke to more than 275 college coaches about tennis, but the topic of the most interest to them was nutrition. Everyone seems interested in diet these days, especially athletes. And rightly so. Nutrition is your number-one fitness factor. If you're not taking in the right fuels, your body will not be up to the demanding exercise involved in playing a tough game of tennis.

If you abuse your body with bad eating habits and excessive use of alcohol or drugs, *you will pay the price.* Make no mistake about that. Your body will be more susceptible to injury, illness, and disease. That's a fact.

My strong recommendation is that if you do nothing else to improve your game, get yourself on a good regimen of healthy eating.

HINTS FOR A HEALTHY DIET

Eating a sensible, varied diet while avoiding empty calories, excessive sugar, and saturated fats, should keep your body working and playing at its best. Here are some basic nutritional guidelines.

1. Eat as many fresh fruits and vegetables as possible. Avoid processed or canned foods—you never know what's in them. If you do buy food that is prepackaged, make sure you read the label. Check for additives like chemical coloring, flavoring, and preservatives—and sugar.

2. Use whole-wheat flour and whole-grain breads and cereals. So-called enriched flour has most of the food value removed and only about one-sixth is replaced. Why take in empty calories—calories with no nutritional value?

3. Avoid added sugar. For example, refined white sugar and foods made with it act destructively on the body, leeching it of vitamins and minerals. Brown sugar is just white sugar covered with molasses. A little honey in recipes isn't bad, but if possible, reeducate your tastes. Sugar is sugar.

4. Swear off junk foods and beverages. It might not be easy, but once you start reading what's actually in these "fabricated foods," it should strengthen your resolve.

5. Be sensible about your intake of saturated fats. Research shows that they contribute to high cholesterol. Saturated fats are usually of animal origin, and some examples are meat, egg yolks, butter, and cheese. This doesn't mean that your diet should be free of all cholesterol and saturated fats—only that you should keep them at a sensible level.

THE VEGETARIAN FUGITIVE

One day in 1971 when I was in between circuits, I was throwing a Frisbee around on the beach in Waikiki with a bunch of my friends and accidentally hit a guy on the head with it. I went over to apologize and we got talking. It turned out he was a doctor and was in town attending a medical symposium on diets, the essence of which was that meat was the worst thing you could put in your body. Oh, no, I thought. Vegetarians!

I have always tried to live by the idea that an intelligent person has an open mind and a closed-minded person learns nothing. But to tell the truth I had a preconceived notion of a vegetarian as a kind of scrawny know-it-all. I remember thinking I wanted to get back to the Frisbee game, but I felt obliged to sit there and listen to this guy because I'd bopped him on the head. So he started drawing charts in the sand and telling me that an athlete should not eat meat six months before an event to perform to his maximum potential. Finally, he persuaded me that I should come to the symposium. But I wasn't exactly convinced.

In the first place, vegetarianism was totally foreign to me. I was brought up a hockey player. A big, juicy, rare steak was a reward and preparation for battle all at once. I needed some moral support. So I went with seven of my friends—five guys and two girls. We showed up at the Hilton Hawaiian Village Convention Hall, where there were three hundred doctors all in suits and ties. And here come eight beach bums—barefoot, wearing bathing suits, and hauling surfboards. We sat way in the back by the door with the surfboards propped up against the wall so we could get out of there fast. We'd all made a deal that as soon as it got boring we'd head back to the beach. Total estimated time was about five minutes.

Five hours later, after dozens of speakers and demonstrations and statistics and studies and tests, after the very last speaker, we finally left. We all went off meat cold turkey and not one of us has touched any meat, fish, poultry, or eggs since. That's how convinced we were.

But the real clincher came when I went to Lloyd Percival's Fitness Center in Toronto, Canada. He had a fitness program in which he tested all of the top athletes in the country. From 1967 to 1969 I was between number fifty and number sixty in the country as a meat eater. The year I stopped eating meat I really wanted to do well in the test because by then I'd become a "vegetarian fugitive." I refused to discuss my eating habits or go out to dinner with anyone because I was embarrassed to be a vegetarian. My parents thought I'd gone off the deep end, and all the players on the circuit constantly ribbed me. I remember I was playing once and Marty Riessen, with whom I played doubles in South Africa, yelled out at me after I missed a ball, "Hey, Burwash, you'd be a lot faster if you didn't have so many carrots hanging out of your ears." And Riessen was one of the nice guys.

So I was very anxious to do well on that fitness test. I had to at least score in the top sixty again so I wouldn't look like a complete idiot, but the cards were stacked against me that day. The day before I had to play in the finals of a tournament in St. Petersburg, Florida. Billie Jean King and Chris Evert were in the women's finals right before me, and they had a long match. Then I got into a long match myself and missed the plane for Toronto. So I got a late plane to Cleveland so I could catch the seven A.M. flight to Toronto. When I got off the plane I went right to the Fitness Center, and I felt the way anyone would feel if they'd slept that night on a bench in an airport—totally exhausted. And the testing procedure was fourteen hours long.

About halfway through the tests this doctor burst into my room and screamed, "What have you been doing?" And I figured, Geez, I've blown it now. But then he said, "You've improved 20 percent in this area and 50 percent in that area and 38 percent in this area." I figured here was another guy who was going to give me static about being a vegetarian, and suddenly he was giving me proof that I was right all along. After a year of being a vegetarian fugitive, those were sweet words.

I had significantly improved my score in every area in which I was tested. And the only change I'd made was in my diet. After one year as a vegetarian I had the highest fitness index of any athlete in the country, and I remained number one every year I was tested.

I wasn't training, I didn't run, I'd just been playing my regular tournament schedule, and I was traveling a lot, which is a great strain on the body. But the testing showed that I was the single most fit athlete of those being tested.

I wanted to present my own experience with a meatless diet to you so that you might give it some thought. At one time vegetarianism was totally foreign to me, and I have always been grateful to the man who introduced me to it. Vegetarianism changed my life, made me healthier, happier, and a better tennis player. It gave me more energy and stamina and a better mental outlook. But it also gave me insights that opened up a whole new way of thinking for me and changed my life in ways I never thought it would.

I personally don't eat any meat, fish, poultry, or eggs—but if this seems extreme, then for the sake of your body at least cut down on your intake.

INDEX